CHARIOTS
of
IRON

50 YEARS

OF

AMERICAN ARMOR

And the Lord was with Judah; and he drove out the inhabitants of the mountain; but could not drive out the inhabitants of the valley, because they had chariots of iron.

Judges 1:19

The quoted passage was used by General Sir Archibald P. Wavell, then commanding British forces in Egypt in 1940, in a message refuting contentions of the War Office that horse and camel cavalry should suffice in desert warfare. His view prevailed, resulting in the formation of the armored force of the British Eighth Army, which was *not* driven out of Egypt. Many of its "Chariots of Iron" were soon manufactured in the United States. These events, as well as the successes of German *Panzers*, spurred the development of U.S. armor.

Experimental T28 assault gun in front of the Patton Museum.

The Board of Trustees of the Patton Museum Development
Fund is honored to present *Chariots of Iron* in commemoration
of the 50th Anniversary of the United States Armored Force.

Martha G. Davis

Mrs. E. L. Davis,
Chairman of the Board of Trustees

3

The M1 Abrams Main Battle Tank.

I am building secure and covered chariots which are invulnerable, and when they advance with their guns into the midst of the foe, even the largest enemy masses must retreat, and behind them the infantry can follow in safety and without opposition.

Leonardo da Vinci

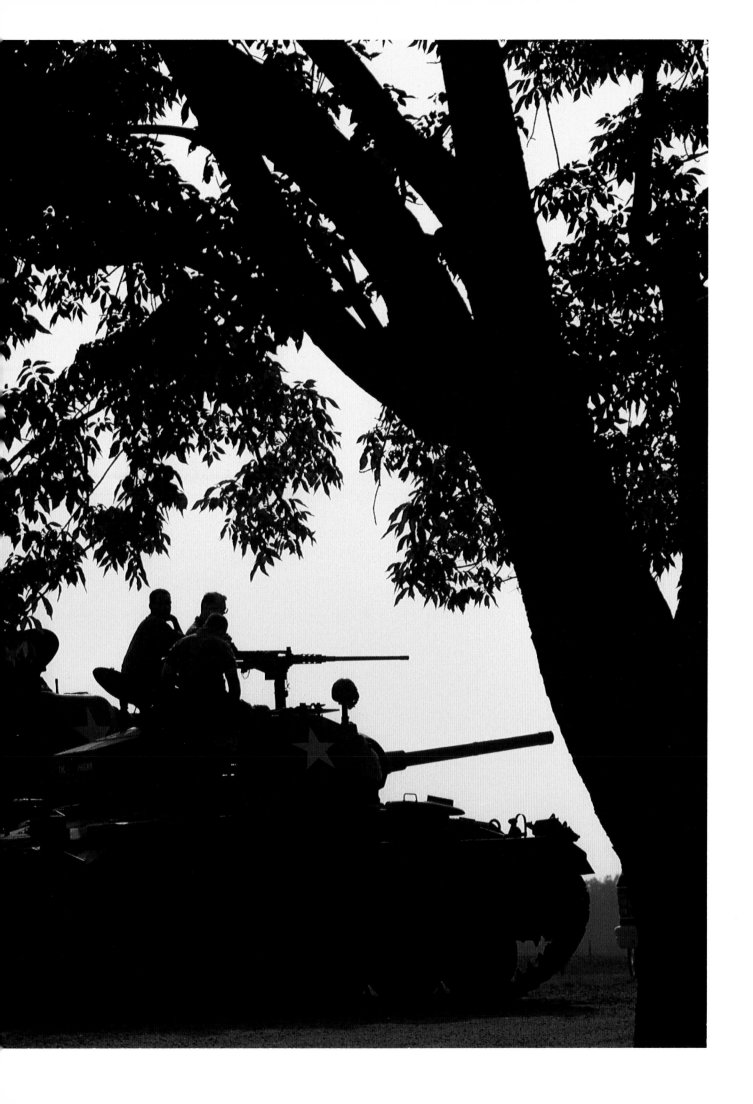

From Gen. J. Lawton Collins, an address at the U.S. Armor Association, January 14, 1952:

I have talked at such length about hardware this morning that I fear that there may have arisen a misconception in the minds of some that equipment is everything. In the Army, however, there is a more important element — the man. . .

To you, officers of all ranks, I look to uphold your heavy responsibilities of leading the finest person in the world — the American soldier.

CHARIOTS
of
IRON

50 YEARS
OF
AMERICAN ARMOR

HARMONY HOUSE
PUBLISHERS LOUISVILLE

Portrait of General George S. Patton, Jr., at
the Patton Museum, Fort Knox, Kentucky

Executive Editors: William Butler and William Strode
Library of Congress Catalog Number: 90-080982
Hardcover International Standard Book Number 0-916509-59-1

First Edition printed Spring, 1990 by Harmony House Publishers,
P.O. Box 90, Prospect, Kentucky 40059 (502) 228-2010 / 228-4446
Copyright © 1990 by Harmony House Publishers

Printed in Canada by Friesen Printers
Through Four Colour Imports, Louisville, Kentucky

The publisher wishes to thank the Board of Trustees, Patton Museum Development Fund: **Officers**: President, Mrs. Emert L. Davis (Martha); Vice President, COL Owsley C. Costlow, AUS (Ret); Treasurer, LTC John K. Volkerding, USAFR (Ret); Assistant Treasurer, Gerald G. Tyrrell; Secretary, LTC John A. Campbell, USA (Ret); Secretary Emeritus, Mrs. Margaret Collier. **Board Members:** Russell Anderson, BG Julius L. Berthold, ANG; BG Philip L. Bolté, USA (Ret); LTC John A. Campbell, USA (Ret); COL Owsley C. Costlow, AUS (Ret); Mrs. Emert L. Davis; COL Ernest L. DeSoto, AUS (Ret); LTC Marshall B. Hardy, Jr., AUS (Ret); COL Edward F. Hessell, Jr. AUS (Ret); Sen. Walter D. Huddleston; Jacques M. Littlefield; MG Thomas P. Lynch, USA (Ret); COL Edward M. Majors, USA (Ret); COL James R. Pritchard, USA (Ret); Edward F. Reed; COL Paul G. Tobin USA (Ret); Gerald G. Tyrrell; LTC John K. Volkerding, USAFR (Ret); Michael W. Wynne and Margaret Collier (Honorary). Special recognition goes to the Book Committee: COL Owsley C. Costlow, Chairman, COL Edward M. Majors, LTC Marshall B. Hardy, Jr., and Edward F. Reed. Finally, special thanks to John Purdy, Director of the Patton Museum; David Holt, Librarian of the Patton Museum; and Major Patrick Cooney, Editor-in-Chief of *Armor* magazine, who were indispensable in the production of this book.

PREFACE

It is a pleasure to participate in the recognition of the 50th anniversary of the Armored Forces, and on this occasion, to offer a few words to those distinguished soldiers who have served in armor since its organization in 1940 during World War II.

My involvement with our branch commenced in 1949 as I transferred from the Infantry to the mobile arm of our Army. Since that time, my service in both peace and war has been with armored and armored cavalry units.

I would trade nothing for this participation, made enjoyable by not only the tank, the Iron Chariot, which is the subject of this volume, but also the magnificent officers and enlisted men who manned, operated, fought, and sometimes died in the performance of their duties. Absent their presence and motivation to move, shoot and communicate in order to "Close with and Destroy," the Chariots addressed in this volume were simply chunks of armor plate lacking life and spirit.

Now the story of these Chariots of Iron and of the band of brothers who manned them is fully related through this excellent documentary.

I offer my most sincere and enthusiastic congratulations to those who are responsible for its production.

George S. Patton
Major General, US Army (Ret)

The United States Army Armor Center Memorial Park, Fort Knox, Kentucky is dedicated to the soldiers who fought with Armor in wars of the twentieth century. This view shows a monument to an Armored Cavalry Regiment that was commanded in Viet Nam by General Donn A. Starry and Major General George S. Patton.

INTRODUCTION

by Donn A. Starry
General, U.S. Army (Ret.)

History records that when "Chariots of Iron" first appeared in battle, they afforded their owners a capability which dramatically decided battle outcomes in their favor. History does not record whether or not the lessons of that battle were sufficiently dramatic to cause the Chariot's owners to rush out and organize an Armored Force so that tactics and techniques — doctrine, organization, and training schemes might be worked out to take full advantage of the Chariot's awesome mobile, survivable firepower. Indeed, what history does recount is that several centuries were to pass before soldiers became prescient enough to understand the battle potential of modern versions of those long-ago Chariots of Iron. In many countries, it was not until the advent of the Industrial Revolution that military thinkers began to contemplate seriously what mobile, survivable firepower could accomplish on battle fields traditionally dominated by masses of infantry and artillery.

This tentative realization was accelerated by events in Europe in the 1930s, and resulted in the creation of Experimental Armored Force organizations in several armies, and at least some preliminary experimentation with modern Chariots of Iron, in various combinations with other arms and services, and in several organizational schemes depending on the prevailing operational thought — usually that of the "senior officer present." In the United States, ocean barrier isolation, a mindset on the rifleman as battle's central actor, and a certain persistent stubbornness among some senior cavalry persons, kept the iron chariot issue very much to the rear of the stove until dramatic successes of the Wehrmacht's Chariots of Iron in the 1939 campaigns in Europe spurred action in the United States. That action of course was set in train by the directive to General Adna Chaffee to organize an Armored Force at Fort Knox, based on the work of the Experimental Armored Force under General Daniel Van Voorhis over the preceding several years.

It is that we memorialize in this book — the occasion of the fiftieth anniversary of the formation of the Armored Force in the United States Army. It is, of course, a force that no longer exists. Having

served its "chestnuts out of the fire" function so successfully in the Second World War, it was considered immediately postwar to be (1) no longer functional in an army without large armor formations, and more importantly (2) a threat to the "turf" of infantry — the rifleman, principal among battle's actors; so it went to the dustbins, the Armored Force.

Time passes, however, and as time will, it more often than not recalls concepts of enduring value — truths that remain both relevant and relatively unchanging. So it is we falter along toward the turn of the century, celebrating as we go, the anniversary of this long-ago perception of the need for an operational identity for the Chariots of Iron, that we find the modern tank — mobile, survivable firepower — linear descendant of the first Chariots of Iron, the tank as the centerpiece of the modern battlefield.

Now and again there rise up detractors who strive mightily to demean the role of armored vehicles in battle. Early on some nuclear zealots put forth the notion that tanks and their companion armored vehicles were likely no longer necessary — for everyone in battle would be done in surely by one or more of the effects of nuclear devastation. Only to find on sober reflection that armored vehicles were not only operable in nuclear war, but were indeed the best machines in which to be embarked in order to survive the "nukes."

Somewhat later, antitank guided missile zealots loudly proclaimed the death knell of the tank. Early in the 1970s, as considerable numbers of antitank guided missile systems were deployed in all armies, word went out that the tank was dead — done in by modern missile technology. Strident voices even proclaimed that staggering tank losses early on in the 1973 Yom Kippur War largely reflected a battlefield dominated by infantry-manned antitank guided missiles. Indeed it required some months of careful evaluation and persuasive argument about what really happened to convince some (but not all) of these people that less than ten percent of tank losses in the Israeli Armour Corps forces in October 1973 were from the highly touted antitank guided missiles.

More recently yet, some technology minded persons are pro-

7th Cavalry Brigade Mechanized, Fort Knox, Kentucky, July 1, 1938. Major General Daniel Van Voorhis commanding.

claiming that top attack weapons — sensor fuzed smart to brilliant munitions — will surely do in the tank at last.

In other arenas, wishful thinkers have seized on the notion that contemporary changes in the Soviet Union and its allies portend that the need for armored vehicles in battle is significantly diminished. In fact, peace is breaking out all over. If indeed peace is breaking out anywhere, it is quite likely a reflection of the more than one hundred thousand tanks of all vintages that comprise the world's contemporary tank fleet inventory — tanks deployed over a wider and wider spectrum of geography, and in the hands of an increasing number of governments/leaders whose political/economic and social stability is frangible at best, and whose political/military intentions escape precise definition and lack some consistency. Therefore it is prudent to conclude it quite likely that the Chariots of Iron not only will survive, but will remain the central actor in battle's Central Duel.

It is not the purpose of this book to recount in detail all of that story — past, present or future. However to the perceptive reader, that story is here, and writ large. So one would hope that this collection of reminiscences, this recital of events, this recounting of the birth and passage of generations of armored vehicles, would invite some considered reflection about our Armored Force history, the biases and prejudices that have worked against it from the beginning, and the enduring character of the Chariots of Iron as the premier, albeit not the only important battlefield system.

Two other important ideas are set forth in these pages. They have to do with the character of the Chariots themselves, and the character of the soldiers and leaders who go to war in the Chariots.

My father enlisted out of college into the Tank Corps in 1917. With the Air Service it was the premier branch to be in — recruiters for both arms worked the college campuses of the nation, enlisting whole athletic teams in several cases, but appealing overall to the brightest and most active young men of the time, wherever they could be found. Tankers of the day trained first at Camp Colt, a place now lost in urban Gettysburg, Pennsylvania. My father's Camp Colt promotion to Sergeant is signed by Captain Dwight D. Eisenhower. Later, in France, he and some of his buddies trained at the Tank Corps School at Langres — its Commandant was Lieutenant Colonel George S. Patton, Jr. And it was Colonel Patton who accompanied, on foot, the U.S. tanks in their first attack across wire and trenches in 1918. Later of course, Captain Eisenhower would become General, and then President Eisenhower. Later still, we would name a whole generation of tanks — M46s, M47s, M48s, and M60s, after General Patton. Like their distinguished namesake, those tanks taught several generations of armor soldiers and leaders all they ever knew about Chariots of Iron. The soldiers, for their part, gave their Chariots names — names like "Avenger," "Dangerous Dan," "Crazy Horse." Like horses of the cavalry, the Chariots took on individual idiosyncracies — ran better after the first fifteen minutes on the march, much better during the last fifteen minutes into the motor park (stable?). Perhaps one of the great literary masterpieces of modern combat is a 1973 poem, written after or during the Yom Kippur War by an Israeli Armoured Corps tank soldier to his tank — tough taskmaster, fierce protector, cranky beast, but always responding to tender care as only the loving can do, saving and sheltering her crew — who love her as she does them.

The Chariots found their everlasting glory in modern battle under command of names like Patton, Wood, Abrams, White, Harmon, Clarke, and many many others equally gifted. In wars other than our own, the Chariots have writ large in battles under command of names like Israel Tal, Musa Peled, Avigdor Kahalani and many others.

Now we have our M1 Chariot — the Abrams. One of General Patton's great warriors in the Second World War, Creighton W. Abrams, Jr., through the Chariot that bears his name, will continue to instruct generations of armor soldiers and their leaders about battle in the Chariots of Iron. Properly so. For it is the unique combination of leaders and the men whom they lead, and the fortuitous marriage of the Chariots of Iron and the iron men who take them to battle that are, and will continue to be, the heart and soul of the Armored Force.

This book is a fitting tribute to the iron men and their Chariots of Iron; it is in modest measure the story of their legacy to us. It is a large legacy indeed.

CHARIOTS *of* IRON
World War I

The development of the modern tank dates, arguably, from the decisive use of armor in the Meuse-Argonne attack of World War I, September 26, 1918. The Tank Corps of the American Expeditionary Forces, formed in January, 1918, rode into that battle in Renault FT17 tanks. (American tank production centered on the six-ton copy of the FT17, and a Ford three-ton, two-man vehicle; neither saw significant action in the war).

By the end of the war, tank engagements numbered almost 100, and armor's authority on the battlefield was established. After World War I, doctrine had the tank in an infantry support role, until men like Adna Chaffee visualized the integration of the tank with cavalry, infantry, artillery and other support arms to form a "combined arms team," a concept that still applies to armor organization today.

The Patton Museum illustrates the early evolution of armored vehicles with its exhibits of the Mark V Star, the Renault FT17, the American Six-ton, and the Ford Three-ton tanks.

A Mark IV "Hyacinth"
caught in a trench, 1918.

British Mark V This large, rhomboid-shaped tank was one of a series developed by the British and used in combat in World War I. It was designed to carry 18 infantrymen in addition to a crew of eight. It was the first of the tanks to have a single driver instead of a steersman for each track. A Ricardo 6-cylinder 150 HP engine powered the vehicle, whose armor plate ranged from .24" to .59" in thickness. Armament included two 6-pounder guns, a .57 mm cannon, and up to eight machine guns on ball-joint mounts.

Renault FT 17 tanks of the 304th American Tank Brigade, commanded by Lieutenant Colonel George S. Patton, Jr., head to Varennes, France in support of I Corps, First Army on September 26, 1918 in the opening battle of the Meuse-Argonne.

U.S. troops in Renault tanks pass a French soldier in the Argonne Forest, 1918.

Two members of the newly-formed U.S. Tank Corps — identified as Sgt. Edward White (above) and Cpl. Edward J. Elliot (driver), both of the 326th/344th Tank Battalion — are seen through the open hatches of their Renault FT 17 tank.

The **Renault FT17** was designed in 1917 as an infantry support vehicle whose principal job was breeching barbed wire and trenches. Its unique feature was a fully revolving turret. A 4-cylinder, 35 HP gasoline engine created a top speed of eight miles per hour. The tank could be armed with a 37 mm cannon, a 75 mm cannon, or a machine gun. American tankers of the Expeditionary Forces went into combat in tanks such as this one. Note: The tank shown above is a 1918 American-built replica of the Renault. Even though this six-ton tank was the standard U.S. light tank for many years after the war, none of the American-built tanks saw any combat with U.S. troops.

A World War I helmet with Tank Corps insignia.

Ford 3-Ton Tank This small, two-man tank was designed and built in 1918 by Ford, using standard Ford automobile parts and two Model T gasoline engines, one for each track. At a top speed of eight miles per hour, this tank was steered by varying the speeds of the two engines. Only 15 of these were built from an original order of 15,000. None of these saw combat in World War I.

CHARIOTS *of* IRON

WORLD WAR II

A tank crew of the U.S. Armored Force in North Africa.

When the German Army moved against France and the Low Countries on May 10, 1940, the United States Army had fewer than 300 armored vehicles of any type. Except for 28 tanks (18 M2 mediums, 10 M2A4 lights), the rest were obsolete compared to German vehicles. Such was the state of mechanization in the U.S. Army. The brief flirtation with armored warfare that began with the U.S. Tank Corps in World War I had advanced little by 1940, despite several attempts to form or experiment with mechanized units in the years between the world wars.

But the events in Europe drove the effort to mechanize, design armored vehicles, and create armored units as quickly as possible. Key figures, among them Van Voorhis, Chaffee, Scott, Devers, Gillem, Patton, Harmon, and Grow, filled the void and spearheaded the new Armored Force, created as a "test" on July 10, 1940. The *Cavalry Journal* of September, 1940 reported: *"On July 10, 1940, the War Department issued an immediate action letter directive creating the Armored Force and assigning Brigadier General (now Major General) Adna R. Chaffee as Chief of the Armored Force and Commanding General of the I Armored Corps. Thus, for the first time, all armored activities of the Army are consolidated for organization, supply and administration under the control of a single commander. Initially, the Armored Force is to consist of the I Armored Corps of two armored divisions and one GHQ Tank Battalion. This represents the Force for which major items of equipment are ready or will be ready by September 1st. It is expected that additional divisions and battalions will soon be formed."*

American industry geared up and began to produce a huge number of vehicles: tanks, halftracks, SP guns, LVTs, and armored cars. In 1943 alone production lines cranked out 29,497 tanks. By 1945 we had produced 28,919 light tanks, 57,027 mediums, and 2,330 heavies. Among the total of 337,388 armored vehicles of all types produced in 1940-45 were some 49,000 M4 Shermans in 20 versions.

By 1945, the U.S. Army had formed 16 Armored Divisions, 71 independent tank battalions, 106 tank destroyer battalions, and 14 amphibious tractor battalions.

— Major Patrick J. Cooney, Editor-in-Chief, *Armor* Magazine

The M4A3E8 — the "Easy Eight" Sherman.

From *Cavalry Journal*, March 1945:

Out of this war U.S. armor has emerged as a powerful arm of opportunity. Using cavalry tactics, armor has exploited the breakthrough made in German lines, plunged forward to disrupt rear echelons, prevented the enemy from reorganizing, cut off his supplies and communications, and spearheaded phenomenal drives into enemy-held territory.

The first decisive breakthrough in which American armor played a significant role occurred during the final days in Tunisia. On May 3, 1943, elements of the 1st Armored Division, commanded by Major General Ernest N. Harmon, broke into Mateur, then quickly fanned out toward Tunis and Bizerte to cut up and surround remnants of the once powerful German Afrika Korps.

In the 38-day Sicilian Campaign in 1943 the 2nd Armored Division, commanded by Major General Hugh J. Gaffey, spearheaded the 72-mile dash from Agrigento to Palermo, reached the Tyrrhenian Sea on July 22, neutralized thousands of German and Italian troops, and prevented any organized resistance on the western third of the island.

In Italy on June 3, 1944, elements of the 1st Armored Division, still commanded by General Harmon, broke out of the Anzio beachhead and spearheaded the advance of the VI Corps, under Lt. General Lucien K. Truscott, through Rome. With Task Force Howze in the lead, the 1st Armored Division then pursued the enemy north until the division was drawn from the line at Volterra on July 10.

As American troops broke out of the Normandy Peninsula in July 1944, the 3rd Armored Division (Major General Maurice Rose, commanding) and the 4th Armored Division (Major General John S. Wood, commanding) spearheaded the phenomenal drives of the First and Third Armies across France to the Siefgried Line.

Now, in March 1945, as new breaks are being made in German defenses — through the Siegfried Line and across the Rhine — armored spearheads are again out front, pursuing, harassing and surrounding a surprised and stunned enemy. To the veteran 3rd and 4th Armored Divisions have been added new armored spearheads — notable, in recent actions, the 6th, 9th, and 11th, commanded respectively by Major General Robert W. Grow, Major General John W. Leonard, and Brigadier General Charles S. Kilburn. The 9th recently led the First Army across the Rhine River into the heart of Germany. The 11th, with the Third Army, spearheaded the drive north along the west bank of the Rhine to join units of the First Army south of Remagen and cut off some 50,000 Germans in the Eifel region. On March 20, the 6th Armored Division, with the Seventh Army, linked up with units of the Third in the Saar region and sealed off another 80,000 Germans doomed to inevitable death or capture.

It is interesting to note that cavalry-trained officers are predominant in these spectacular actions.

M2A3 Light Tank The M2A3 was known as a "cavalry" tank. Except for the double turrets, it is essentially the same as the M1 Combat Car (later called the M1 Light Tank). It was introduced in 1938, and was powered by a 7-cylinder radial aircraft engine. Armaments included one .50 caliber machine gun in the left turret, two .30 caliber machine guns in the right turret, and one .30 in the bow.

M3A1 Scout Car The last of the wheeled, open-top armor vehicles. 20,000 of these were produced. By the end of the war the halftrack and the M8 Armored Car had replaced the M3A1. A 6-cylinder gasoline engine supplied power to all four wheels. Armor plate was .25" thick. It could be armed with either .30 caliber or .50 caliber machine guns; this particular version has a .50 in the bow, a .30 to the rear. The roller in the front was used as an assist in ditch crossing.

Medium and light tanks of the 1st Armored Division in a mass front formation at Fort Knox, 1941. Vehicles include M2 and M2A1 medium tanks (front row), M2A3 tanks (second row), and M1 Combat Cars.

From Col. Hayden A. Sears in March 1947 *Armored Cavalry Journal:*

It is apparent in any review of World War II that, in all theaters, on all types of strategic terrain, under a wide range of climatic conditions, and in varying types of operations (land, water, and air), armor not only played its part, but without it, conclusive successes were seldom achieved. Further consideration also reveals that in continental operations of major magnitude, strategic successes were never achieved without the powerful contributions of armor employed in a spearhead role.

M2A2 Light Tanks (also known as "Mae West" tanks for their twin turrets) are shown during maneuvers at Fort Sam Houston, Texas in 1937.

From January 1944 *Cavalry Journal*:

One of the 1st Armored Division halftrack ambulances came racing up to the crossroads just south of the Anserine Farm, and the driver, with the "valor of ignorance," instead of turning left, kept on straight toward the farm. This road had been used only as far as the crossroads. Dust generally would bring fire, but it was long-range and very inaccurate—never closer than 200 yards to a jeep. When fire got that close the driver would detour through the wheat and poppy fields.

As the ambulance rolled on toward the farm, observers kept field glasses on it and held their breath. If the German fired, his exact location would be known. The ambulance stopped at the farmhouse, turned quickly around, and came out a lot faster than it went in. The observers stopped the ambulance, and when the medical officer could talk, he informed them that he thought he had been moving to the rear instead of toward the front; that, as his vehicle approached the farmhouse, a German soldier had stood up beside a well camouflaged antitank gun and asked in English if there were any wounded in the ambulance. The doctor couldn't recall his answer, but the driver had turned the ambulance around and wheeled it away.

In addition to obeying the Geneva convention, the German apparently knew that if he exposed his gun by firing at anything less than a tank he would catch one hell of an artillery concentration!

A mechanized column of Scout Cars moves through a stream on maneuvers at Fort Knox, 1939.

The M2 Halftrack was designed for use as a primemover of 105 mm howitzers by Field Artillery (armored) regiments and battalions. It was considered an excellent cross-country vehicle at the time.

M3A1 Light Tank (Stuart) Between March 1941 and September 1943, nearly 14,000 of these were made. The A1 version pictured here had a more streamlined turret than earlier models. The crew was protected by armor up to 1.5" thick, and employed a 37 mm gun in the turret and three .30 caliber machine guns.

M3A1 light tanks of the 2nd Armored Division in formation, 1941.

A tank platoon from the 1st Armored Division on maneuvers in Louisiana, 1941. Observers are judging how well the tanks are using the woods in the background to dim the tank silhouettes.

From Lt. Col. E.A. Trahan in May 1947 *Armored Cavalry Journal:*

The morning of October 6, (1944) dawned gray and wet, and under the lowering clouds the Third Battalion (67th Armored Regiment of 2nd Armored Division) launched yet a third attack. At 8 a.m. an artillery serenade was placed on every known enemy strongpoint, and simultaneously the tanks rumbled forward. They were met by withering fire. Direct fire from Mark V and Mark VI tanks was added to the increased weight of artillery, antitank, mortar, and small arms. Movement outside of the protection of the tank's armor was suicidal, so concentrated and sustained was the weight of the enemy fire. The M-4's gradually withdrew to the jump-off leaving a trail of blazing and knocked-out hulls behind them. Another attack of the medium tanks was obviously impossible.

But perhaps speed would succeed where power had failed. C Company was composed of 17 M-5 light tanks, armed with 37mm guns — weapons which would worry the heavily armored German tanks no more than a mosquito sting ... But the M-5's had one thing the Germans did not have — speed. And in this one advantage their commander placed his hope.

Gathering themselves, the light tanks burst through the lines of mediums at 11 a.m. on the morning of the 6th, throttles wide open and the prayer of every man in the line riding with them. At 35 miles per hour, the M-5's screamed toward the enemy in a single weaving line. The German gunners must have thought them mad. Then, as the realization dawned that they could not track these fleeting targets in their sights, the seeds of panic were sowed. The tankers and infantry who were to follow watched in wonder. One thousand yards, and not a tank hit. Two thousand yards, and still not a gap appeared in the charging line. The Germans were firing every weapon they had, and the line was alive with stabbing flashes, but the light tanks seemed to bear charmed lives. Individual Germans began to run to the rear. But every gun in the swiftly advancing line was firing, and they were cut down before they fairly started.

... In its attack C Company destroyed two batteries of artillery, several antitank guns, and numerous smaller arms. It made possible the capture of several pill boxes, much material, and over 200 prisoners. It had routed a full platoon of vaunted German Mark VI tanks, and had advanced the American line almost 2,500 yards. This it had done with weapons and armor vastly inferior to that of its opponent. The disparity was made up in gallantry, skill, and raw courage.

M3A3 Medium Tank (Lee) This tank was jointly designed by the U.S. and Great Britain in 1940. The A3 version shown here had welded armor up to 2" thick. Two GM 6-cylinder diesel truck engines supplied power to a 5-speed transmission. Steering was via a handbrake applied to either track. The standard six-man crew used a 75 mm gun, a 37 mm gun in the turret and three .30 caliber machine guns.

From Maj. A.J. Wilson in March 1947 *Armored Cavalry Journal*:

Particularly up to the end of the Tunisian campaign, and to a slightly less degree afterwards, armored forces were without doubt the dominant arm on land during the 1939-45 war. The German onslaught of Poland, the collapse of France, the German victories in Russia in 1941 — all these were due in the last resort to the power of armored forces. Warfare in the Western Desert and in Tunisia mainly also followed this trend, though towards the end of the period the dominance of armor on both sides was greatly reduced by the improvement in the caliber and performance of anti-tank weapons. Nevertheless the dominance of armor was reflected in the concentration with which commanders at all levels studied their tank "runner" states, and it became second nature to base a plan on the quantity and quality of armor available on either side. Infantry were reduced at least in their own minds if not in those of their commanders to the status of "tank followers," and were relegated to the roles of holders of a firm base and "moppers up" of pockets of resistance which had been by-passed or otherwise neglected by the all-dominant armor.

The Battle of Alamein and the stiff, dour fighting of the Tunisian campaign did much to redress the balance, which in Italy during the Winter campaigns of 1943-44 and 1944-45 even became tilted toward infantry as the dominant arm. Nevertheless, as soon as the sun shone and the mud of the Winter and early Spring developed into the dust of early Summer, it was to armor that commanders, whether in Western Europe or in the Mediterranean theater, looked for their decisive successes. The advances in Italy from Cassino to Florence (1944) and the Senio to the Alps (1945) were both predominantly armored operations after an initial infantry dogfight, while in France and Germany the pursuits from Falaise to the Seine and Scheldt and from the Rhine to the surrender on Luneburg Heath were equally operations in which armored formations played the leading role. It is thus evident that armor was the dominant arm on land during the late war, even if many of its successes could not have been achieved without a previous victory in the infantry battle.

M3 medium tanks on the range at Fort Knox, 1941.

The M4 Sherman.

M4 Sherman The main U.S. battle tank of World War II and Korea. Probably the most prolific tank ever produced, with about 50,000 built since 1942. Early models were first used in North Africa, where its 3" armor and 75 mm gun were competitive with German Mark III and Mark IV tanks. Its 31 tons of weight can reach top speeds of 25 MPH. The standard, five-man crew consists of the driver, bow gunner, gunner, loader, and commander. It was an extremely reliable vehicle, and saw combat in many versions over the years, including "Flails," tank dozers, bridge-layers, flamethrowers, rocket carriers, and recovery vehicles.

From COL Owsley Costlow:

The attack would cross the line of departure at first light. It would be our entire Battalion in the assault with my Platoon leading. We had been briefed that Tiger, Mark VI Tanks, and 88mm anti-tank guns had been reported in the vicinity and that a sister Tank Battalion (43rd) had been almost eliminated the day before. I was not looking forward to this day!

My specific mission was to drive on the dug-in German Infantry positions, move them out of there, stop and pick up friendly Infantry (66th AIB) and attack the small town of Offendorf, France on the Rhine River. Intelligence had assured us that there were only "old men and young boys out there and that they all wanted to give up." Later we discovered it was the 10SS Panzer Division and they never gave up!

The town of Herrlisheim was on our left flank, Stainwald Woods, a large forest, was on the right. Our job was to go in between.

We had come up that night and now were in position waiting in the dark for the sun to rise. Radio listening silence was in effect. The code word to begin the attack was "Zippo." The sun came up; all shadows had disappeared; we were in a large, open field. We were ready, but no "Zippo." It became mid-morning with us just sitting there exposed. I ran back to the Company Commander's tank; he said he was waiting on Battalion. Surely all the element of surprise was gone now so if anyone was out there in front of us they most certainly knew we were there.

At around 1045 the silence was shatttered by "Zippo" — move out at your own speed. I ordered the Platoon forward by sections, one overwatching the other while we moved up by leaps and bounds. Through my binoculars I could see many unmanned M4 Shermans "parked" in very strange positions. I radioed to my Captain telling him what I saw and he said they were from the day before. Then, I saw several long-coated infantrymen get up out of a foxhole, move very quickly to another hole, and drop out of sight. They were always moving facing us but it was still too far away to see clearly who they were. They did have on long coats, were facing us, and they were not within .30 caliber machine gun range. I again radioed my Commanding Officer asking him if everything in front of me was enemy. He replied, Yes. Then I requested permission to begin firing. "Permission granted!" Gunner, doughs (dismounted infantry) 800 yards, direct front, 30 caliber, fire! "On the way" was given by the gunner and the trigger pressed, but the solenoid that fires the coaxial machine gun had slipped and did not engage the trigger. Immediately, the loader began to adjust the solenoid as the tank continued to move forward. I was still watching the front through my binoculars and to my horror I now began to see that those doughs were our own Infantry — GI's moving from hole to hole. Cease fire! Cease fire! The Good Lord was there, Divine intervention for sure! Our solenoid had never failed before nor did it after that time. That is something I have thought about many times since.

A World War II tanker's helmet.

Horizontal Volute Suspension System (HVSS) was the last suspension system used on the M4A3E8 Shermans at the end of World War II.

An early M4 Sherman being tested at Fort Knox. Note the fixed machine guns in the bow, left/right driver vision ports, and the three-piece transmission cover.

M4A1 Sherman of the 1st Armored Division in Italy, late 1944.

From Joseph Morschauser in March 1960 *Armor* magazine:

The Japanese private opened fire. In a few minutes, the Americans were pinned to the ground and artillery fire began to rake their positions. The GIs could not move and could not hurt the Japanese in their deep, well-prepared positions, and in a few moments more the cry crackled out over American radios. "Hey, Zippo, come on!"

Shortly several M4 Sherman tanks ground forward, their dull green hulls shaking off small arms and artillery fire. The Japanese stopped one by smashing its drive sprocket with a 47mm antitank slug but the others avoided the gun's fire and crawled up to the face of the escarpment. The tanks sprayed cave entrances with .30 caliber slugs. But the Japanese were no longer there. They had withdrawn deep into their holes, safe from the machine guns' fire.

Down in the cave the Japanese private smiled nervously, thankful he was safe from the tank's fire. He knew that even a 75mm high explosive shell could not reach him there. Then suddenly, his place of safety became a flaming trap. As his companions collapsed, the private tore out his gas mask and ran for the entrance of the inferno. As he emerged into daylight, his clothing aflame, tracers cut him down. Operation Blowtorch had begun.

An M4 Sherman fitted with an E-4 Series flame gun.

The **M10 Tank Destroyer** was a new generation of the T35 which began development in 1942. Five thousand M10s were built between September, 1942 and December, 1943. The 30-ton vehicle had a top speed of 30 MPH. A second version, the M10A1, such as the one shown here, of which 1400 were built, used the M4A3 chassis. A further development, the M36, used a 90 mm gun in response to the results of the Normandy tank battles. The M36 was introduced in the European theater in late 1944.

One of the 704th Tank Destroyer Battalion's M18 Tank Destroyers.

The M36 Tank Destroyer, with 90 mm gun.

From May 1944 *Cavalry Journal*:

Tank destroyers are provided with light armor as a protection against small arms, machine guns and fragments. Tank destroyers should never attempt to fight as tanks, since their armor is not designed to withstand antitank weapons. It is interesting to note, however, that the M-10 destroyer has armor characteristics which make it comparable to the German Mark III and Mark IV tanks, both of which have proven themselves extremely capable in their role.

In discussing equipment, no reference has been made to the auxiliary weapons and the reconnaissance and general purpose vehicles, since they are similar to those of other arms. In summation, attention is called to the requirements laid down for the tank destroyer as a weapon. To quote General A.D. Bruce, who commanded the Tank Destroyer Center from its inception until May, 1943:

"What we are after is a fast moving vehicle, armed with a weapon with a powerful punch which can be easily and quickly fired, and in the last analysis, we would like to get armored protection against small arms fire so that this weapon cannot be put out by a machine gun."

The M5 Halftrack.

The suspension system on the M5 Halftrack.

M32 Tank Recovery Vehicle, manufactured from the M4 chassis.

The M8 Armored Car.

Self-propelled 105 mm gun-howitzer M7. The version shown above, designated the B1, was modified during the Korean conflict to permit high-angle fire. Note the added height of the frontal armor and of the round machine gun sponson — from which shape the British in World War II nicknamed this weapon the "Priest." The M7 was the most ubiquitous piece of artillery armor in World War II.

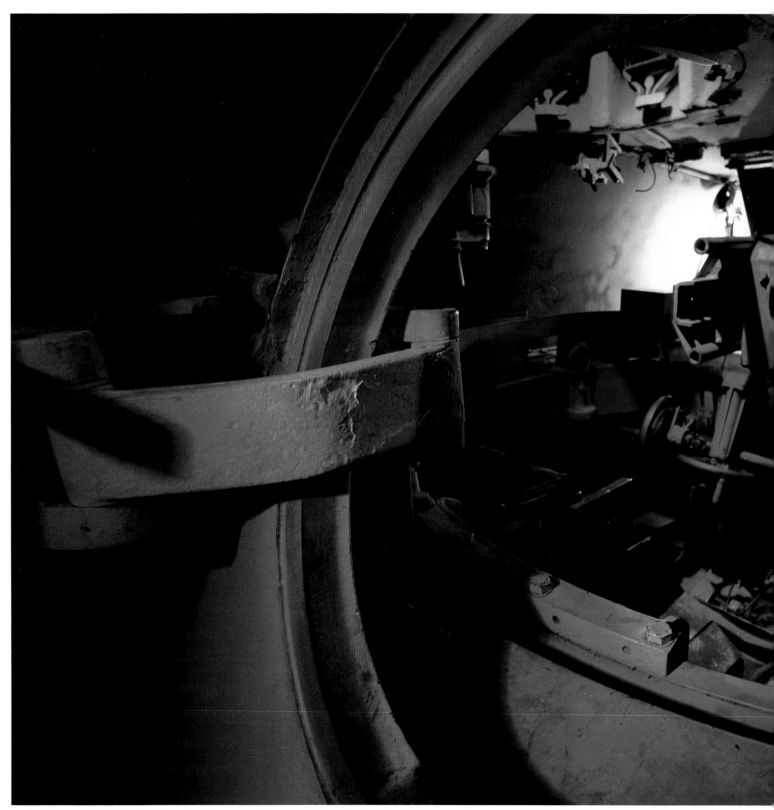

Inside the turret of a German Panther tank. This version is a Panther II prototype with a Panther I turret. The Panther II was to have an 88 mm gun, and MG 34 machine guns in the bow and turret.

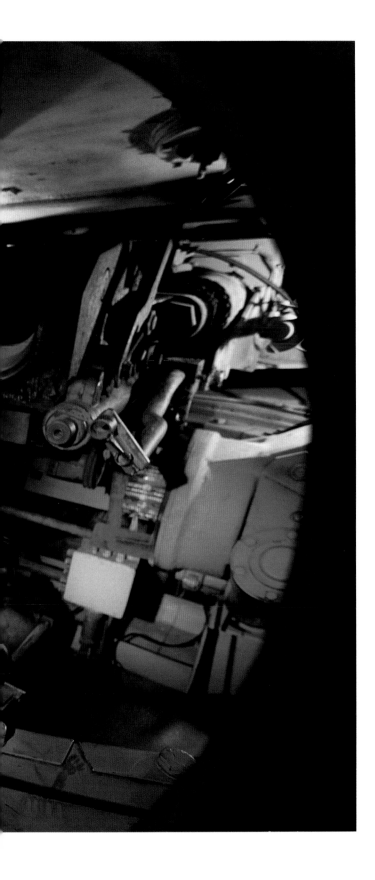

From Major John North in September 1944 *Cavalry Journal:*

The armored thrusts in France by Lt. Gen. Patton's Third Army have been true enveloping movements, perfectly conforming to the old cavalry tradition from the point of view of disrupting enemy communications, and of isolating enemy concentrations. It is in the amplitude of their conception, in their depth, and their wide dispersion that these great wheeling thrusts have made military history. They have brilliantly demonstrated what can be achieved by such thrusts against a widely dispersed and insufficiently mobile enemy. They have extinguished at a blow Germany's far-from-mythical "Atlantic Wall." They have vindicated General Patton's own battle creed, "Attack rapidly, ruthlessly, viciously, and without rest." They have achieved the apotheosis of armor.

Tanks of the American Third Army pass a knocked-out German tank on the road to La Chappelle as they chase the retreating German army.

The M24 Light Tank "Chaffee" was first used in Europe in the latter months of 1944, and saw action in the Pacific theater as well. Production on this tank began in April 1944; 3300 were produced in the U.S. The five-man standard crew utilized a 75 mm gun, two .30 caliber machine guns and one .50 caliber machine gun. Its 18.1 tons could reach a top speed of 34 MPH.

CHARIOTS *of* IRON

KOREA

An American tank crew, Korea, 1952.

Korea was our first "come-as-you-are" war, and we were not dressed very well.

At the time of the North Korean attack across the 39th parallel on June 25, 1950, World War II demobilization had emaciated the massive Armored Force of 1945. By mid-1948, there were only 10 Regular Army divisions still on the rolls. Of those, the 2nd Armored was the only armored division.

The armored force immediately available to throw against the North Koreans was minute by anyone's definition. In Japan, the 7th, 24th, and 25th Infantry Divisions, and the 1st Cavalry Division each had one company of M24 "Chaffees" — the A Company of the 77th, 78th, 79th, and 71st Tank Battalions, respectively.

Though fighting courageously, the M24s were no match for the firepower or armor protection of the North Korean Soviet-built T43/85s. Rushed to Korea in July and August were the 6th, 70th, 72nd, 73rd, and 89th Tank Battalions. These battalions averaged 69 tanks each: the 6th had 90 mm M26 Pershings, and the others were evenly composed of M46s and M4A3E8 "Easy Eight" Shermans. The M46 was essentialy an M26 with a better gun, new engine, and cross-9-drive transmission. By the end of August, the United States had about 500 tanks in Korea. In November the 64th Tank Battalion entered the war as part of the 3rd Infantry Division.

The war spawned the production of the M103 (120 mm gun) heavy, the M47 (90 mm gun) and M48 mediums, and the M41 (76 mm gun) light tanks, even though they were not fielded in the Korean conflict.

The war prompted the activation of the 1st, 3rd, 5th, 6th, and 7th Armored Divisions, and the 11th Armored Cavalry Regiment, although none deployed to Korea.

— Major Patrick J. Cooney, Editor-in-Chief, *Armor* Magazine

The M24 "Chaffee"

M26 Pershing Tank The M26 was designed in 1942 to utilize torsion bar suspension rather than springs, and as such it was a significant departure from Sherman configurations. Limited numbers were issued during World War II, but it became the U.S. main battle tank thereafter, until 1950. The tank shown above was used in the Korean conflict. Armor plate is up to 4" thick, and the tank is powered by an 8-cylinder gas engine. Its 90 mm gun was competitive with German tanks, and also carried two .30 caliber machine guns and one .50 caliber machine gun.

A Cessna spotter plane flies over advancing tanks and infantry near Heartbreak Ridge.

From Lt. Willard A. Colton in May 1953 *Armor* magazine:

In Korea the tankers have learned a new lesson: How to climb ridges and fight from mountaintops.

Tankers first took to the hills in force in the Mundung-ni Valley in December, 1951, when the 31st Infantry Regiment launched a bunker-busting operation. The Japanese had always built bunkers on the lower slopes of hills, where they could get good grazing fire across the valley floor. But the Chinese Reds build their bunkers at the military crest and on the ridgetops; they are dug into rock, with log-and-dirt walls three feet thick. Tanks can't hit them effectively from the valley.

So the commander of the 31st decided to put his tanks where they could fire right into the enemy's teeth. In three days the 13th Engineer Combat Battalion slashed a road up the rear slope of Hill 605 — about 1,000 feet straight up. Then four tanks were moved into position on top of the hill. The platoon leader spotted them where they could cover a battalion front, and dug them in so only the turrets were visible. Within a week fifteen Chinese bunkers had been knocked out. Bunker-building by the Chinese on their forward slopes came to an abrupt halt.

A typical M46 tank emplacement in Korea.

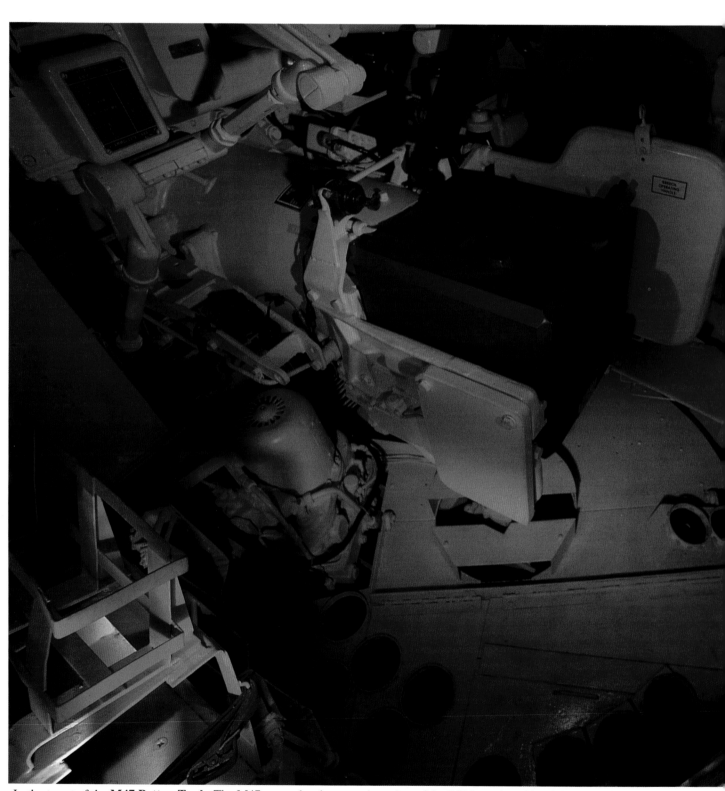

In the turret of the **M47 Patton Tank**. The M47 was a developmental version of the M46, produced in 1951. The hull of the M46 was retained, but the commander's cupola was improved. The main gun is a 90 mm cannon, complemented by two .50 caliber machine guns (one mounted coaxially with the cannon), and a .30 caliber machine gun in the bow. The high-velocity gun is fitted with a fume extractor and blast deflector. Some models had an optical rangefinder and a ballistic computer.

From Captain Sam Freedman, September 1952 *Armor* magazine:

The tank tactics at Heartbreak Ridge offer a case in point. The major tank attack was "Operation Touchdown," so named because it involved a long end-run around the left flank of the enemy at Heartbreak to strangle his line of communications which had its apex at the northern entrance to the Mundung valley. It was a vigorous, penetrating thrust, brilliantly planned and daringly executed. Every tanker in the battalion rode to the attack in 68 Shermans loaded with HE and hypershot, and carrying extra ammunition for the battalion of the 38th Infantry marching along to nail the antitank squads.

The big thrust, which took place on October 10, 1951, marked the finish of enemy action at Heartbreak Ridge. Any plans the Reds may have had to counterattack again for that prized ridge, were rendered "kaput" by the 72d's tankers. The troops of the 38th, 23rd, and 9th Infantry regiments, aided by United Nations battalions, had finally shattered enemy resistance on that blood-drenched mountain. The tankers had finally broken through, after heroic work by the 2nd Engineers to prepare the way for them through a winding creek bed of the Han River.

The attack itself came at a most opportune time. It caught the Reds completely off stride. The results were all that had been intended. Alert 2nd Division and X Corps Intelligence were aware that approximately a division of fresh Chinese troops, hastily recruited and trained at Tientsin, was to replace the decimated North Korean Red forces at Mundung-ni, about six miles north of Heartbreak Ridge.

The tank column took off at 0600 on a split-second schedule, guided from an OP far to the front, where two 72nd Tank Battalion staff officers had set up a radio relay station. From this point the officers could observe the floor of the Mundung valley, report the presence of enemy forces, guide the tanks into action, and bring down supporting fires as needed.

A tank is just the place for a man who likes hard slugging. You've got a good, big gun, and can move it handily where it will do the most good. The hardy lads of the 72nd, enjoying the action after their long wait while the Division engineers were smoothing down the route, virtually stuck those tubes down the throats of the Reds and made them say "ah."

The **M41 Bulldog** was introduced in 1950. It was later renamed the Walker Bulldog for General Walton Walker, killed in Korea in 1951. It was an improved version of the M24. It saw little use by the U.S. in combat, but was the main battle tank of the South Vietnamese army. It was the first U.S. tank to employ a single-unit powerpack (engine and transmission as one unit). Features of the M41 are a 76 mm gun, hydraulic fire control, and a fast turret reverse.

As was often done in Korea, this tank serves as mobile artillery from a prepared, camouflaged position.

Two M4 Sherman tanks pull a disabled tank into a smoke screen to cover its withdrawal during Operation "Blaster."

CHARIOTS *of* IRON

VIETNAM

M48 Patton Tank Produced in 1953 after development stages of the M46, M47, T42 and T43 tanks. The M48A3 became the mainstay of the U.S. tank force until the development of the M60. These tanks featured a 90 mm cannon, one .50 and one .30 caliber machine gun, and a crew of four.

On March 9, 1965, the 3rd Platoon, Company B, 3rd Marine Tank Battalion drove its M4A3 tanks onto the beach at DaNang and became the first U.S. armored unit to deploy to Vietnam. The prevailing attitude for several years was that, except for a few coastal areas, the terrain in Vietnam was no place for armored vehicles. But as they were gradually introduced to Vietnam, armored and mechanized units demonstrated a capacity to maneuver in most terrain and a usefulness far greater than anyone predicted.

The first Army armor and cavalry units deployed to Vietnam in 1966. With their M113 APCs and M4A3 tanks, early armored units had to experiment with tactics and techniques, which coincided with the evolution of airmobile operations. Armored units served as the fixing force, while airmobile infantry maneuvered against the enemy. The armored force, led by tanks, had sufficient combat power to take on the massive ambush long enough to bring artillery, air, and infantry assets to bear.

In early 1969 a new vehicle, the M551 "Sheridan" received its introduction to combat. It replaced the M48 tanks in the cavalry platoons of divisional cavalry squadrons and the M113 ACAVs that had been substituted for tanks in the cavalry platoons of regimental cavalry squadrons.

By the cease fire in January, 1973, U.S. armored units had participated in every large-scale offensive operation during the war. Through participation in operations like CEDAR FALLS and JUNCTION CITY, and the battles of Khe Sanh and Hue City, Army and Marine cavalry and armor units added to their already considerable prestige.

— Major Patrick J. Cooney, Editor-in-Chief, *Armor* Magazine

M113 Armored Personnel Carrier.

From Lt. Col. Raymond R. Battreall, Jr., May 1966 *Armor* magazine:

At first glance, Armor tactics in Vietnam may seem highly unorthodox. If you will consider what has been said about the various vehicles, however, you will see that the APC has simply assumed the orthodox role of the main battle tank. By the same token, the light tank has, in those areas where it can operate, taken on the role of the main battle tank supporting the actions of the M-113 by heavy firepower and, where possible, adding weight to the assault. With these substitutions in mind, standard doctrine becomes applicable. Armor in Vietnam, as presently equipped, is capable of the full range of normal armor operations. It performs best, however, when employed on offensive missions in close cooperation with Infantry. The ultimate tactical objective of the Vietnamese trooper is to physically overrun the enemy and crush him beneath his tracks. All of his efforts are directed to this end, and the psychological — or "shock" — effect on the enemy of this armor equivalent to "the spirit of the Bayonet" is very great indeed.

M113 APC with Vietnam-style armor protection at gun stations.

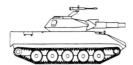

Heavy-dropping an M551 Sheridan.

From Col William B. Cobb, March 1967 *Armor* magazine:

Though the enemy should have learned that the Blackhorse Regiment strikes back hard and fast, he obviously did not. Late in the afternoon of 2 December near Xuan Loc he attacked a convoy escorted by two tanks and two ACAVs. An estimated Viet Cong Regiment hit the small unit and the reaction was devastating. The tanks poured round after round of canister and machine gun fire into the jungle while the ACAVs delivered thousands of rounds of machine gun and grenade fire with deadly accuracy into the bewildered ranks of the VC. With the precision of a well-oiled machine the troopers maneuvered their vehicles within the killing zone, rooting out the VC from their fortified positions as the reaction force was converging on the ambush site. The fighting continued as darkness fell and went on throughout the night as the remainder of the squadron closed in on the enemy with the support of tactical air, flare ships, and artillery. Morning light disclosed 99 dead Viet Cong. Numerous small arms were captured: a 75mm recoilless rifle, rocket launchers, a 60mm mortar, one heavy and three light machine guns, countless grenades and small arms ammunition and other military equipment. The casualty figures for the Regiment clearly demonstrated the value of armor protection. The Blackhorse had no KIA's, and only a few wounded, most only slightly. Both actions showed that even when struck in ambush, Armor can absorb the initial blow and return effective fire immediately.

M551 Sheridan The Sheridan replaced the M41 as the U.S. light reconnaissance vehicle. It is fully amphibious, and has airborne capability. The hull is welded aluminum, the turret, steel. Weaponry includes the "Shillelagh" guided anti-tank missile plus a variety of 152 mm ordnance, a 7.62 mm coaxial machine gun, a .50 caliber machine gun, and eight grenade launchers. 1700 Sheridans were produced from 1959 through 1966.

Sheridan drops from a C-130 on a low-altitude parachute extraction maneuver.

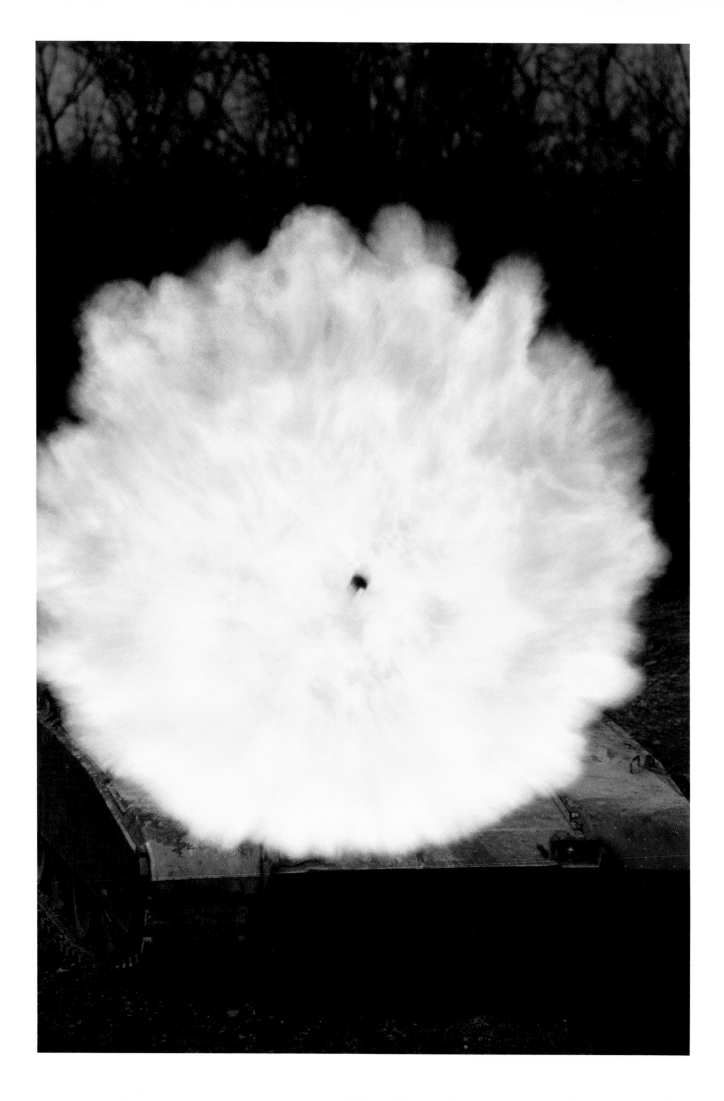

CHARIOTS *of* IRON

TODAY

A Cobra helicopter guards the right flank of an advancing M1 tank.

Unlike its predecessor of a half-century ago, which scrambled to organize and train in the face of an overpowering aggressor, today's Armor Force is the most potent in the world.

Mounted on M1 "Abrams" series tanks, our first new tank in decades, today's tanker can shoot further with greater accuracy than ever before. Coupled with its stablemate, the M3 "Bradley" Cavalry Fighting Vehicle, our tank and cavalry teams can move, shoot, and communicate with unmatched speed and lethality.

But, as much as the technology and hardware of armored warfare have changed over the last five decades, the role of armor has remained as Chaffee envisioned it in the 1930s: to close with the enemy and defeat him through the trained use of firepower, maneuver, and shock effect. The force is manned by highly trained, motivated, professional, volunteer soldiers who consider themselves an elite group able to meet any challenge anywhere in the world.

Armor is still the centerpiece of the mobile, combined arms team, and will continue to be the "Combat Arm of Decision" well into the next century.

— Major Patrick J. Cooney, Editor-in-Chief, *Armor* Magazine

The M60, the last of the "Patton" series, was the U.S. main battle tank for over three decades.

M60 series tanks begin deployment (above); advance in line (above right); and take position (below right).

The M1 Abrams Main Battle Tank.

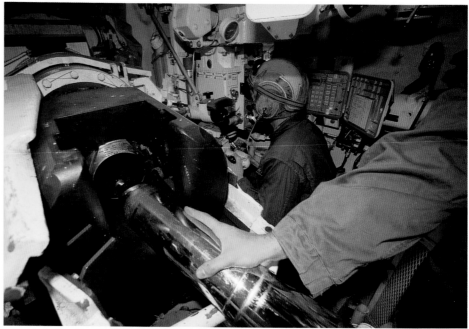

Inside the turret of the M1.

Bird's eye view of the M1 Abrams.

An M60A3 and an M113 APC on maneuvers.

This is the M1 gunner's view of a target through his thermal imaging sight, which converts temperature variations into two-dimensional pictures.

An M1 firing sequence...

The M3 Bradley (left) and the M1 Abrams MBT (right).

A Cobra attack helicopter overwatches a convoy of M113 APCs.

An M60 with search light. Although commonplace years ago, the M1 Abrams and its thermal imaging sight has rendered this configuration virtually obsolete.

The M2 Bradley at work.

The Apache Attack Helicopter, part of today's combined armor team.

The Cobra Attack Helicopter, a vital air-mobile arm of the armor team.

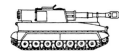

M109A2 Howitzers.

M109A2 Howitzers firing in support.

"Humvee" (HMMWV) with TOW missile launcher.

Armored Combat Engineer Vehicle M9 (ACE).

M113 APC with TOW missile launcher.

M60 Armored Vehicle Launched Bridge.

M88 Recovery Vehicle.

"To me, World War II is a 30-ton tank. A stinky, noisy, crowded, overheated (or freezing cold), bone-shaking iron coffin. For 33 months overseas with the 2nd Armored Division, this tank was my principal home and transportation.

In this tank I watched life and death happen in ten different countries. I sweated through the heat of Africa and the freezing cold of Belgium during the Battle of the Bulge. I got wet every time it rained.

From this tank aboard an LCT (Landing Craft Tank) I watched as the worst storm in 50 years hit the Mediterranean Sea as we were on our way to invade Sicily. Our little LCT was tossed like a cork, and all but two of us were so seasick we didn't care whether the storm sank our boat or the Germans did.

From this tank, I watched the fields of Sicily erupt into a sea of white surrender flags as the Italian Army gave up by the hundreds and thousands.

In this tank on June 10, 1944, I rode up onto the beaches of Normandy, France, and again saw the wreckage of war — the dead and dying lying in the fields around Carentan, friend and enemy side by side. The weary paratroopers had been fighting for a week, and they cried as we handed them belts of ammunition. They were down to fighting with bayonets and knives. Their ammunition was gone.

From this tank I watched the grateful people of France, Belgium and Holland give us flowers and liquor as we liberated their homes from the Germans.

From this tank I waved goodbye to a high school buddy for the last time. We met by chance in a field in France during a three-hour lull in battle. Three weeks later he was dead.

From this tank I watched an American soldier get up from the ground after an enemy shell exploded next to him. He slung his rifle over his shoulder and walked back to my tank saying, "The dirty SOBs shot my arm off. Where are the medics?" I pointed to the rear and he just kept on walking, holding on to the stub of his arm.

Near this tank I talked to two little old German women, who were sitting on the steps of their apartment building. They were so glad the Germans retreated from their town, and no shots were fired by either side. The war was nearly over. Then, one last German antitank crew decided to take a shot at my tank. They missed. But the shell hit one of the women and she was blown to bits. The other looked on in disbelief as her own leg rolled down the steps.

Yes, from this tank I watched many events and I still remember..."

— From Arden Gatzke, originally printed in the *Milwaukee Journal* in 1975, and reprinted in the 2nd Armored Division book, *Roll Again Second Armored.*

1st Armored Division

BATTLE CREDITS
(European-African-Middle Eastern Theatre)

Algeria/Morocco   Tunisia   Naples/Foggia   Rome/Arno   North Apennines   Po Valley

COMMANDERS
(World War II era)

July 1940 to March 1942	MG Bruce Magruder
March 1942 to April 1943	MG Orlando Ward
April 1943 to July 1944	MG Ernest N. Harmon
July 1944 to September 1945	MG Vernon E. Prichard
September 1945	MG Roderick Allen

COMPONENT UNITS

As of May, 1942: 1st and 13th Armored Regiments; 6th Armored Infantry Regiment, 27th, 68th and 91st Armored Field Artillery Battalions. *Reorganized July, 1944*: 1st, 4th and 13th Tank Battalions; 6th, 11th and 14th Armored Infantry Battalions; and 27th, 68th and 91st Armored Field Artillery Battalions. *High Commands (Combat)*: II Corps (North Africa); Fifth Army (Italy).

The "Old Ironsides" Division was activated on 15 July, 1940 at Fort Knox, Kentucky, largely from redesignated units of the 7th Cavalry Brigade (Mechanized). It trained at Fort Knox for 20 months, with major maneuvers in Arkansas, Louisiana and South Carolina in 1941. Units of the Division developed such important equipment as the tank dozer, armored radio vehicles and the surgical truck. It moved to Fort Dix in April of 1942, in preparation for departure in two groups to Northern Ireland in May, 1942. The Division shipped to England in late October, 1942, prior to battle commitment of CCB and CCA in North Africa in November and January, respectively.

1st Armored Division World War II Combat History

Combat Command B of the 1st Armored went into action first in the invasion of North Africa, landing near Oran on 8 November, 1942, and securing the city two days later. Within two weeks, elements of CCB were attacking with the British Blade Force more than 700 miles to the east near Tunis. Then in "Stuka Valley" (Tine River) and the "Mousetrap" (Medjerda Valley), those elements held off counterattacks by the 10th Panzer Division before helping the French in the Ousseltia Valley. CCA fought first at Faid Pass. It was decimated by Rommel at Sidi Bou Zid, and both Commands fought at Kasserine Pass, from which the Division attacked toward Maknassay in March. In late April the Division shifted over 100 miles north, driving on Mateur, capturing it on 3 May and continuing to the Mediterranean near Bizerte, taking 23,000 prisoners and receiving the unconditional surrender of the 5th Panzer Army from its commander on 9 May, 1943. After a period of reorganization, re-equipping and training for future operations, the Division re-entered combat in Italy. On 9 September, 1943, two small elements of the Division took part in the landings at Salerno and Paestum; the remainder of the Division arrived in Italy in November, and by mid-December was committed in the Gustav Line fighting. Units of Task Force Allen (General Frank Allen, Jr. of Combat Command B) attacked and took Mt. Porchia by 9 January, 1944, but suffered heavy losses in doing so. By the end of January CCB had been detached from the Division and continued its role in the battle for Cassino. The rest of the Division landed on the Anzio beachhead. For four months its job became primarily defensive, containing German assaults and counterattacking, notably on 19 February, 1944. The Division began the offensive breakout and drive toward Rome on 23 May, 1944. The fighting was fierce and tank losses were heavy through 29 May beyond Campoleone Station. Against continuing resistance, the Division pushed forward toward Albano and the Highway 7 route to Rome, while its Task Force Howze advanced on Highway 6. Elements of the 1st entered Rome on 4 June, 1944. The Division continued its pursuit of the retreating Germans, taking Viterbo on 9 June. Passing into 5th Army reserve for a much needed rest, the Division was back in action on 22 June, leading the attack toward the Arno River. For virtually the next year, commencing with the battle at Casole d'Elsa and ending in late May of 1945 at Milan, the 1st fought across Italy in heavy, bitter fighting. The battle line followed a path from Mount Pisano through Altopascio, Lucca, Castelvecchio, Mt. Liguana, and Ponte a Moriano before settling into an October-long battle at Monterumici. Surging forward again in late 1944, the Division swept through Carviano, Salvaro, Suzzano and Vergato in the drive to the Swiss border. The Division broke into the Po Valley in April, 1945, and crossed the Po River 26-27 April. By 30 April, the Division had taken Milan and was driving north to Cigliano when German forces in Italy capitulated on 2 May, 1945. Old Ironsides performed occupation duties until relieved, sailing for the U.S. on 16 April, 1946.

The 1st Armored closes in on Rome, June 3, 1944.
Here an M7 gun crew awaits the clearing of snipers
on the road ahead.

Tanks of the 1st prepare for the push into the Po Valley in
the spring of 1945.

1st Armored M4 tank in the "Mousetrap" operation in the Tine River valley.

A 1st Armored tank at the crossroads between Mateur and Tunis.

This 1st Armored tank rolls through Ponsacco, Italy, en route to Volterra in the summer of 1944.

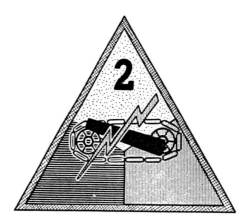

2nd Armored Division

BATTLE CREDITS

Algeria/French Morocco   Sicily   Normandy   Northern France   Rhineland   Ardennes   Central Europe

COMMANDERS
(World War II era)

July 1940 to January 1941	MG Charles L. Scott
January 1941 to February 1942	MG George S. Patton, Jr.
February 1942 to July 1942	MG Willis D. Crittenberger
July 1942 to April 1943	MG Ernest N. Harmon
April 1943 to May 1943	BG Allen F. Kingman
May 1943 to March 1944	MG Hugh J. Gaffey
March 1944 to September 1944	MG Edwin H. Brooks
September 1944 to January 1945	MG Ernest N. Harmon
January 1945 to June 1945	MG Isaac D. White
June 1945 to September 1945	MG John H. Collier
August 1945	MG John M. Devine

COMPONENT UNITS

As of September, 1942: 41st Armored Infantry Regiment; 66th, 67th, Armored Regiments; 14th, 78th, 92nd Armored Field Artillery Battalions. *Higher Commands*: First, Fifth, Seventh and Ninth Armies.

The "Hell on Wheels" Division was activated at Fort Benning, Georgia on 15 July, 1940. It took part in the major maneuvers of 1941 in Tennessee, Louisiana, and South Carolina, and then in North Carolina in 1942. In the summer of 1942 it moved into bivouac at Fort Bragg, North Carolina from where its units rotated through the Navy Amphibious Center in Norfolk, Virginia. On the beaches of the Chesapeake the Division practiced assault landings. On 8 November 1942, elements of the Division began the 2nd's combat record in North Africa.

2nd Armored Division World War II Combat History

Elements of the Division first entered combat in North Africa, landing at Casablanca, 8 November, 1942, and later taking part in the fighting at Beja, Tunisia. The Division as a whole, however, did not see action until the invasion of Sicily when it made assault landings at Licata and Gela on 10 July, 1943. It pushed inland to Butera, then west along the coast to Campobella where it swung north across the island to capture Palermo on 23 July, 1943. After the Sicilian campaign, the Division moved to England to train for the cross-channel invasion. It landed at Omaha Beach, Normandy 9 June, 1944, and went into action at Carentan. It broke through the German St. Lo-Vire River Line at St. Gilles 26 July, attacked south to St. Hilaire, then raced east to cross the Seine River 28 August. It was the first allied division to enter Belgium, driving over the border at Rumes on 2 September, 1944, and continued its advance through the German Albert Canal Line and over the German border at Schimmert on 18 September. It then took up defensive positions at Geilenkirchen until it resumed the attack against the Siegfried Line on 30 October during which it knocked out more than 70 pillboxes of Hitler's "impregnable west wall" and crossed the Wurm River, seizing Puffendorf on 16 November and Barmen on the 28th. At the outbreak of the Battle of the Bulge, the Division raced 75 miles southwest from its positions along the Roer River to eastern Belgium where it blunted the German 5th Panzer Army's penetration. Then battling through the deep snow of the Ardennes Forest, it helped reduce the German salient in January and cleared all enemy in the area from Houffalize to the Ourthe River. After a brief rest, the Division once more moved up to the front on 26 February, 1945, drove across the Rhine, and raced on to make contact with 1st Army units and seal off the Ruhr pocket on 1 April. Without losing momentum, it swept eastward, and was the first American Division to reach the Elbe River. It crossed the river on 11 April, 1945 at Schonbeck south of Magdeburg and then halted on orders. It was relieved and moved back into reserve. In July, it claimed credit to another "first" when it was the first American unit to enter the German capitol of Berlin. It remained in occupation until it departed in January, 1946, for the United States and Fort Hood, Texas.

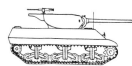

CCA of the 2nd Armored Division moves through the town of Valkenburg, Holland.

2nd Armored rolls through Ahlen.

A tank of the 67th Armored Regiment enters the village of St. Sever Calvados.

These tank destroyers of the 702nd TD Battalion fire across the Roer River.

3rd Armored Division

BATTLE CREDITS

Normandy   Northern France   Rhineland   Ardennes   Central Europe

COMMANDERS
(World War II era)

April 1941 to January 1942	MG Alvin C. Gillem
January 1942 to August 1942	MG Walton H. Walker
August 1942 to August 1944	MG Leroy H. Watson
August 1944 to March 1945	MG Maurice Rose
March 1945 to June 1945	BG Doyle O. Hickey
June 1945 to July 1945	BG Truman O. Boudinot
July 1945	BG Frank A. Allen, Jr.
July 1945 to November 1945	MG Robert W. Grow

COMPONENT UNITS

As of August, 1945: 32nd and 33rd Armored Regiments; 54th, 67th and 391st Armored Field Artillery Battalions; 36th Armored Infantry Regiment. *Higher Command*: First Army.

The "Spearhead" Division was activated at Camp Beauregard, Louisiana on 15 April, 1941, and two months later moved to Camp Polk, Louisiana when construction of that post neared completion. It remained at Camp Polk until July, 1942, when it left for Indio, California and training in desert conditions. In November it was transferred to Camp Pickett, Virginia. Two months later it went on to Indiantown Gap, Pennsylvania where it continued to train until departure for New York. Embarkation for England began on 4 September, 1943.

3rd Armored Division World War II Combat History

The 3rd Armored Division landed on Omaha White Beach in Normandy, 23 June, 1944, and, six days later, was committed at Villiers Fossard. After a slow fight through the hedgerows, it broke out at Marigny on 26 July and swung south to Mayenne in a general exploitation of the St. Lo breakthrough. From there, wheeling east and north, the "Spearheaders" participated in the drive which, on 18 August, closed the Argentan-Falaise gap around the German Seventh Army. Seven days later, the Division cut across the Seine River, and began streaking through Meaux, Soissons, Laon, Mons, and Namur. Continuing the eastward push, it seized Liege on the 8th of September and Eupen on the 11th, fought into the Siegfried Line with the capture of Rotgen on 12 September and, against heavy resistance, advanced slowly to Langerwehe and Hoven on the Roer River. When the Battle of the Bulge broke, the Division shifted southwest where it severed a vital highway leading from Manhay to Houffalize and, in January, helped reduce the German salient north of Houffalize. After a brief rest, the 3rd Armored returned to the front, broke out of the Duren bridgehead and drove east to capture Cologne on 6 March, 1945. It swept on to Marburg, then north around the Ruhr Valley. In the vicinity of Etteln, south of Paderborn, in the afternoon of 30 March, lead elements of CCB, followed closely by General Rose, the Division Commander, were suddenly caught in the fire of marauding German Panther and Tiger tanks in the woods on both sides of a narrow dirt road down which the combat command was attacking. While trying to run the ambush, the General's jeep was pinned against a tree by an enemy tank. In the melee, the German tank commander opened fire with a machine pistol on the General and his party, killing General Rose. Paderborn was secured the next day and, when contact was made with the 2nd Armored Division attacking down from the north, the Ruhr pocket was sealed off. On 5 April, the "Spearhead" soldiers resumed the attack eastward, crossed the Saale River 13 April and, after overcoming stiff resistance, cleared Dessau by 23 April. Two days later, the Division pulled back into reserve, then performed occupational duties, following VE Day, until inactivated on 9 November, 1945.

A 3rd Armored tank pauses in Huchin, Germany.

The 3rd leaves Stumsdorf, Germany in flames.

This anti-aircraft crew of the 3rd Armored near Bastogne searches the sky for enemy planes.

This 3rd Armored tank rolls past a knocked out German tank near Marienburg, Germany.

Generals Eisenhower, Montgomery and Watson inspect the 3rd Armored training area in Wilts, England, 1943.

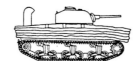

4th Armored Division

BATTLE CREDITS

Normandy   Northern France   Rhineland   Ardennes   Central Europe

COMMANDERS
(World War II era)

April 1941 to June 1942	MG Henry W. Baird
June 1942 to December 1944	MG John S. Wood
December 1944 to March 1945	MG Hugh J. Gaffey
March 1945 to June 1945	MG William M. Hoge
June 1945 to August 1945	BG Bruce C. Clarke
August 1945 to September 1945	BG William L. Roberts

COMPONENT UNITS

As of December, 1943: 10th, 51st and 53d Armored Infantry Battalions; 8th, 35th and 37th Tank Battalions; 22nd, 66th and 94th Armored Field Artillery Battalions. *Higher Commands*: First and Third Armies.

The 4th Armored Division was activated on 15 April, 1941 at Pine Camp, New York, and trained there until participating in the Tennessee maneuvers of 1942. From mid-November, 1942 until June, 1943 it underwent desert training in California, then transferred to Camp Bowie, Texas. The following December it moved to Camp Miles Standish, Massachusetts. Embarkation for England followed from Boston on 29 December, 1943.

4th Armored Division World War II Combat History

The 4th Armored Division landed at Utah Beach on 11 July and saw its first action on 17 July. Moving through the St. Lo breach on 28 July, it drove south, seized Coutances the same day, and fought on to take Nantes 12 August and cut off the Brittany Peninsula. Turning east, it sped across France north of the Loire River, took Orleans on 16 August, crossed the Seine and captured Troyes on 25 August, then raced across the Moselle 13 September, encircled Nancy 15 September, and seized Luneville 16 September. After maintaining the defense line Dhambrey-Xanrey-Henamenil from 27 September to 11 October, the Division was relieved but returned to the front on 9 November with an attack in the vicinity of Viviers. It cleared the Bois de Serres on 12 November, advanced through Dieuze, crossed the Saar River on 23 November, then took Singling and Bining on 8 December. Two days after the Germans launched the Ardennes offensive, the 4th Armored was ordered northwest to help relieve the encircled forces at Bastogne. It broke through the German ring and continued the fight to reduce the enemy salient until suddenly pulled out of the line on 15 January, 1945 to prepare for another anticipated German attack from the Trier area. In late February, after failure of the attack to materialize, the Division jumped off again, and plunged over the Moselle at Trier, driving south and east to Worms and across the Rhine on 24 March 1945. Advancing all night, it crossed the Main River south of Hanau the next day and continued on to take Lauterbach 29 March. Creuzburg across the Werra fell 1 April, Gotha on the 4th and, by the 12th, the Division had crossed the Saale River. Pushing on to the east, it drove to within two miles of Chemnitz before being relieved on 16 April. It retired to an area near Bayreuth but was on the move once more on 1 May. It wheeled southeast toward Czechoslovakia and, on 6 May, attacked through friendly units toward Prague. It established a bridgehead across the Otara River at Strakonice and had pushed forward elements to Pisek at the war's end. On 26 May the Division moved back into Germany to assume occupation duties in the Regensburg area until inactivated and reconstituted as part of the constabulary forces in Germany.

General Patton with 4th Armored commander MG John S. Wood at the front, October, 1944.

The 4th moves at double-time.

On the road to Bastogne. Sherman tanks of the 4th Armored Division deploy in a clearing near Sainlex, Belgium during the Battle of the Bulge.

September 2, 1944. The 4th rolls through St. Amand, France.

The 4th Armored Division takes Avranches, July 31, 1944.

5th Armored Division

BATTLE CREDITS

Normandy   Northern France   Rhineland   Ardennes   Central Europe

COMMANDERS
(World War II era)

October 1941 to February 1943	MG Jack W. Heard
March 1943 to July 1945	MG Lunsford E. Oliver
July 1945 to September 1945	BG Morrill Ross
September 1945 to October 1945	MG Holmes E. Dager

COMPONENT UNITS

As of February, 1944: 15th, 46th and 47th Armored Infantry Battalions; 10th, 34th and 81st Tank Battalions; and 47th, 71st and 95th Armored Field Artillery Battalions. *Higher Command*: Third Army.

The "Victory" Division was activated on 1 October, 1941 at Fort Knox, Kentucky. Five months later it was sent to Camp Cooke, California. Training in desert conditions in the Mojave Desert began in August of 1942 and continued until November. The Division shipped from Camp Cooke, in March of 1943, to Tennessee for maneuvers there. It was then shipped to Pine Camp, New York from July to September, and on to Indiantown Gap, Pennsylvania from December to February, 1944. Finally the Division moved to Camp Kilmer, New Jersey before final deployment to New York, and on to England on 10 February, 1944.

5th Armored Division World War II Combat History

The 5th Armored Division landed at Utah Beach 22 July, 1944, and saw its first action north of Fougeres on 2 August. It joined in the 3rd Army breakout from St. Lo, driving south through Coutances, Avranches, and Vitre, then east across the Mayenne River to seize LeMans on 8 August. Swinging north to forge a ring around the German 7th Army in Normandy, it reached Argentan on 12 August, six days before the Argentan-Falaise Gap was closed. Turning its positions over to the 90th Infantry Division, it then raced 80 miles east to seize Dreux and secure crossings over the Eure River on 16 August. Two days later, the "Victory" 5th pushed to the Seine River to form a second enemy entrapment in France. After helping to clear the Eure-Seine pocket, it drove northeast from Paris through the Compiegne Forest and, in rapid order, seized Compiegne on 31 August and Noyen on 2 September, then sped on past St. Quentin and Cambral to cross into Belgium at Conde late that same day. It turned its positions over to other U. S. units, then moved south and resumed the attack eastward on 4 September. By mid-afternoon, it reached Charleville-Mezieres on the Meuse, crossed the river the next day against strong resistance, pushed on to take Sedan 7 September, then fought into Luxembourg to liberate the capital on the 10th. Fanning eastward from the city, the division secured the first allied foothold on German soil by dusk the next day, crossing the border at Stalzenburg. It continued driving to seize Wallendorf on the 14th and, by evening of 15 September, had penetrated the Siegfried wall through the line of scattered pillboxes. It was relieved by the 8th Infantry Division on 2 October, but returned to the front late in the month and, in November and December, joined in the fierce Huertgen Forest fighting. In January and February, it helped eliminate the Ardennes salient and drive the enemy back to the Roer River. On 24 February, it crossed the river, and spearheaded the XIII Corps push to the east. It seized Rhiendahlen 27 February, cutting off Munchen-Gladbach, then raced on to the Rhine. It held briefly west of the river, then moved north, passed through the 9th Army bridgehead at Wesel on 31 March, and drove on to cross the Weser River on 8 April. Attacking rapidly to the east, it seized Rohrberg 12 April and on the the 13th reached the Elbe at Tangermunde, just 45 miles from Berlin — the point of closest advance to the German capital reached by any allied unit on the western front. After being ordered to hold at the river, the Division conducted mop-up operations in the 9th Army sector, then performed occupation duty after VE Day until its return to the States.

The 5th Armored in Linhof, late April, 1945.

CCA of the 5th crosses the Weser River at Hameln, April 9, 1945.

The 5th clears the town of Tangermunde.

Early March, 1944. The 5th in convoy near Rasseln.

6th Armored Division

BATTLE CREDITS

Normandy   Northern France   Rhineland   Ardennes   Central Europe

COMMANDERS
(World War II era)

February 1942 to May 1943	MG William H. Morris, Jr.
May 1943 to July 1945	MG Robert W. Grow
July 1945 to September 1945	BG George W. Read, Jr.

COMPONENT UNITS

As of January, 1944: 128th, 212th and 231st Armored Field Artillery Battalions; 15th, 68th and 69th Tank Battalions; 9th, 44th and 50th Armored Infantry Battalions. *Higher Command*: Third Army.

The "Super Sixth" Division was activated on 15 February, 1942 at Fort Knox, Kentucky. In March, the new Division moved to Camp Chaffee, Arkansas for five months prior to the Louisiana maneuvers in August and September, 1942. After a brief return to Camp Chaffee the Division embarked for Camp Young, California to participate in Desert Training Center maneuvers from October 1942 to March 1943. In the middle of March, the Division moved to Camp Cooke, California, remaining there until being moved to Camp Shanks, New York. It embarked from New York on 10 February, 1944, and arrived in England on 23 February, 1944.

6th Armored Division World War II Combat History

The 6th Armored Division landed at Utah Beach 18 July, 1944 and entered combat near Millieres on the 27th. Passing through the 79th Infantry Division in the St. Lo breakthrough, it drove through Avranches, then swung west to help liberate Brest and clear the Brittany Peninsula. On 13 August, it extended its deployment to relieve the 4th Armored Division and assume the added mission of containing the fortress of Lorient. Later, the "Super Sixth" was given a further mission of protecting the south flank of the 3rd and 9th Armies, resulting in a front responsibility of 460 miles from Brest to Auxerres when finally relieved on 17 September. Moving to eastern France, the Division assembled in the Luneville area and was recommitted, 8 November, in an attack toward the Saar. It reached the river and had pushed the enemy back to the Siegfried Line by 23 December, when ordered north of Metz to assist in cutting off the German salient at its base with an attack toward St. Vith along the west bank of the Our River. Striking the southern shoulder of the penetration, it helped in thwarting the enemy's withdrawal to the Siegfried Line. Then, after a brief respite in late January it rejoined the offensive and bridged the Our River 7 February, preliminary to a major attack on 20 February against the German "west wall". By evening of the 21st, it had cleared the last Siegfried defenses, then pushed east to cross the Prum River 27 February, and the Nims River 2 March. It was relieved at this point and moved south to the Chateau-Salins area below Metz where, on 20 March, it once more assumed the offensive. Passing through the 3rd Infantry Division near Zweibrucken, it attacked northeast and, by 0900 the next day, had driven 60 miles to the Rhine at Worms. It crossed the river at Oppenheim on 25 March behind the 4th Armored Division and continued the push northeast, forcing a bridgehead over the Main River at Frankfurt 26 March, seizing Bad Nouheim 29 March, then bypassing Kassel to capture Mulhausen and Langensalza on the 5th and 6th of April respectively. Veering right, it attacked eastward to liberate the infamous concentration camp at Buchenwald on 11 April and reached the Mulde at Rochlitz on 5 April. It held at the river on orders, then went on the defense and conducted mop-up operations for the remainder of the war, after which it performed occupation duties until it returned to the States.

A 6th Armored Division tank negotiates the hedgerows, watchful for German opposition.

A familiar and well-remembered sight to Super Sixers.

A 6th Armored tank hides in the rubble of Suisse, France, November 18, 1944.

A rocket-equipped tank of the 6th Armored patrols near Wichte, Germany.

A Sherman with a hedgecutter maneuvers at speed around a defeated German artillery piece.

7th Armored Division

BATTLE CREDITS

Northern France Rhineland Ardennes Central Europe

COMMANDERS
(World War II era)

March 1942 to November 1944	MG Lindsay McD. Silvester
November 1944 to August 1945	MG Robert W. Hasbrouck
August 1945 to September 1945	BG Truman E. Boudinot

COMPONENT UNITS

As of June, 1944: 434th, 440th and 489th Armored Field Artillery Battalions; 17th, 31st and 40th Tank Battalions; 17th, 31st and 40th Tank Battalions; 23d, 33th and 48th Armored Infantry Battalions. *Higher Commands*: Third Army, British Second Army, First Army and Ninth Army.

The "Lucky Seventh" Division was activated at Camp Polk, Louisiana on 1 March, 1942, remaining there one year, participating, meanwhile, in the 1942 Louisiana maneuvers from September to November. Further training and maneuvers in desert techniques followed at the Desert Training Center from March to August, 1943. After that it took up station at Fort Benning, Georgia until being shipped to Camp Miles Standish, Massachusetts on 22 April, 1944. Departure for New York began on 7 June, 1944, and arrival in England was completed by 14 June, 1944.

7th Armored Division World War II Combat History

The 7th Armored Division landed in Normandy on 10 August, 1944 and immediately joined in the pursuit of the Germans across France. Driving east it took Chartres on 18 August, crossed the Seine and took Melun on the 24th, captured Chateau-Thierry on the 25th, then pushed on, encircling Rheims and seizing Verdun and crossings over the Meuse on 31 August. After a brief halt, it resumed the attack, reached the Moselle River at Dornot on 7 September, and joined a bridgehead at that point two days later. It drove on to the Seille River against heavy resistance, then was relieved on 23 September and moved to Holland where it cleared the enemy in the Paul Swamp region west of the Meuse. On 8 October, though still part of the U.S. 1st Army, it was placed under operational control of the British 2nd Army to provide right flank protection for the British-Canadian drive on Antwerp. On 7 November, it returned to U. S. Army control and assembled in the vicinity of Geilenkirchen to prepare for an attack across the Roer River. However, the Germans struck first with their Ardennes offensive and the division was ordered south to the St. Vith area where, with CCB of the 9th Armored Division and elements of the 106th Infantry Division, it held that vital sector until forced west of the Salm River on 23 December. It shifted its defenses to Manhay and later, on 23 January, while the Germans were being pushed back, it retook St. Vith. It subsequently assisted the 9th Infantry Division in the drive to the Rhine and, upon seizure of the Remagen Bridge by the 9th Armored Division, it deployed along the west bank from Born to Unkelbach to block any enemy effort at destruction of the crossing by river infiltration from the north. On 24 March, the Division crossed the Rhine and, passing through the bridgehead, attacked east to take Giessen on the 28th, then swung north to seize both the Edersee Dam and crossings over the Eder River on the 29th. After assisting in the reduction of the Ruhr Pocket, it was relieved 17 April and moved north to Celle where, as part of the U.S. XVIII Corps attached to the British 2nd Army, it crossed the Elbe River and launched an attack over the Mecklenburg Plains toward the Baltic Sea on 3 May. Contact with the Russians was made later that day after which the division conducted mop-up operations followed by occupation duty until return to the United States four months later.

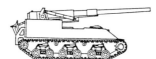

A portion of the Siegfried Line, spring, 1945.

The 7th pursued retreating Germans through France, here at Dourdan.

On a road near Verdun, a reconnaissance patrol of the 7th Armored searches for enemy artillery positions.

A 7th Armored division tank commander rounds up German prisoners in Ruhr Pocket action near Fruelinghausen, Germany, April, 1945.

A German Mark V swept to the side of the road by the advancing 7th Armored, near St. Vith.

8th Armored Division

BATTLE CREDITS

Rhineland   Ardennes   Central Europe

COMMANDERS
(World War II era)

April 1942	BG Thomas J. Camp
April 1942 to September 1944	MG William M. Grimes
October 1944 to July 1945	MG John M. Devine
August 1945 to November 1945	BG Charles F. Colson

COMPONENT UNITS

As of November, 1944: 18th, 36th and 80th Tank Battalions; 7th, 49th and 58th Armored Infantry Battalions; 398th, 399th and 405th Armored Field Artillery Battalions. *Higher Commands*: Fifteenth, Third and Ninth Armies.

The "Thundering Herd" Division was activated with a cadre training mission at Fort Knox, Kentucky on 1 April, 1942. The Division was initially called the "Iron Snake," but subsequently adopted the "Thundering Herd" moniker and another, its war code name of "Tornado." After nine months at Fort Knox, it moved south to Fort Campbell, Kentucky, where in February, 1943, it was relieved of its cadre training mission and directed to attain combat-ready status. In March the Division moved to North Camp Polk, Louisiana, and began training for combat service. In October, 1943, it moved from garrison to bivouac and conducted extensive field exercises, followed by the Louisiana maneuvers from February to April, 1944. It then returned to South Camp Polk, remaining there until departure for Camp Kilmer, New Jersey in late October, 1944. Departure for New York began on 7 November, with arrival in England on 18 November, 1944.

8th Armored Division World War II Combat History

After training for almost two months at Tidworth, England, the 8th Armored landed in France 5 January, 1945 and assembled in the vicinity of Pont-a-Mousson, France, to organize a counterattack against an expected enemy strike in the Metz area. On 22 January, after failure of the German attack to materialize, the Division joined the fighting in support of the drive by the 94th Infantry Division against the enemy's Saar-Moselle salient. Six days later, it was relieved and moved north to the Maastricht, Holland area to prepare for participation in 9th Army's attack toward the Rhine. It crossed the Roer 27 February and assisted the 35th and 84th Infantry Divisions in their push eastward, taking Tetelrath, Oberkruchten, Rhienberg, and Ossenberg against stubborn resistance. Following a brief rest, the Thundering Herd crossed the Rhine at Wesel 26 March and attacked east to help form the northern arm of the Ruhr Valley encirclement. Taking Dorsten and Marl on 29 March, it crossed north of the Lippe Canal on 1 April and raced east to reach Neuhaus on the 3rd. At that point, it veered south, then attacked west into the Ruhr Valley in an effort to help eliminate the Ruhr Pocket. In mid-April, when the XIX Corps drive to the Elbe was threatened from the south, the division was pulled out and rushed east to provide right flank protection against fanatical remnants of the German 11th Panzer Army grouping in the Harz Mountains. Assembling in the vicinity of Halberstadt, it attacked south against the German force, taking Blankenberg on the 20th of April, and seizing Ottenstedt on the 21st in the division's last coordinated action of the war. It continued mop-up operations and performed occupation duty in the Harz Mountain area up to and immediately following VE Day. Then, in late May, it was ordered south to Czechoslovakia to assist in processing prisoners of war, operating displaced persons camps and guarding vital installations including the Skoda Munitions Works. The Division closed in the Pilsen area 6 June, 1945 and remained there until departure 19 September for return to the United States and inactivation at Camp Patrick Henry, Virginia, on 13 November, 1945.

8th Armored Division tanks in formation for repair and maintenance, spring, 1945.

On January 24, 1945, 8th Armored troops, after scarcely three weeks in France, take German prisoners near Berg.

The streaking 8th takes more prisoners near Roermond, February 26, 1945.

Occupation duty for the 8th Armored in the Harz Mountain area, 1945.

9th Armored Division

BATTLE CREDITS
Rhineland   Ardennes   Central Europe

COMMANDERS
(World War II era)

June 1942 to September 1942	MG Geoffrey Keyes
October 1942 to October 1945	MG John W. Leonard

COMPONENT UNITS

As of August, 1944: 27th, 52nd and 60th Armored Infantry Battalions; 2nd, 14th and 19th Tank Battalions; 3rd, 10th and 73rd Armored Field Artillery Battalions. *Higher Command*: Third Army.

The "Phantom" Division was activated at Fort Riley, Kansas, on 15 July, 1942, incorporating many elements of the famous 2nd Cavalry Division, and including the 3rd Field Artillery Battalion which traces its history back to the American Revolution. On 10 June, 1943, the Division moved to Goff, California and on to Camp Ibis, California on 1 August, 1943. Camp Polk, Louisiana was the next stop in late October to participate in the Third Army No. 5 Louisiana maneuvers. It was staged at Camp Kilmer, New Jersey, from 14 August until departure for New York on 18 August, arriving in England 1 September, 1944.

9th Armored Division World War II Combat History

Division combat elements entered the line along Luxembourg's eastern border on 23 October, 1944 and, at the outbreak of the Ardennes offensive on 16 December, the three combat commands, due to their wide dispersion along the VIII Corps front, were forced to fight separately. To the north, CCB, practically alone, held the vital town of St. Vith for 36 hours, then continued to fight with the 7th Armored Division after its arrival in that area. In the center, CCR, with one of the most difficult missions in the Ardennes, slugged it out against overwhelming odds and, though suffering heavy casualties, including the loss of all three battalion commanders, was officially credited with delaying the enemy east of Bastogne for 48 hours before falling back to fight with the 101st Airborne Division. To the south, CCA held a sector in the Beaufort area against everything the Germans threw at it until relieved to join the 4th Armored Division in breaking a corridor through to Bastogne. Following a rest after the Bulge, the Division crossed the Roer River on 28 February, attacked southeast to take Euskirchen 4 March, and seize crossing over the Ahr by noon on the 7th. Later that day, Task Force Engeman changed the entire complexion of the war by seizing the Ludendorff Bridge at Remagen. One large charge, which partially damaged the bridge, detonated as lead elements of the task force started over the first span, but advancing against murderous fire and tearing out other charges as they raced to the far bank of the Rhine, they secured the bridge at 1550 hours, just ten minutes prior to scheduled destruction. Attacking east and south out of the bridgehead, the Division captured Limburg 26 March, liberating thousands of allied prisoners in the first POW camp to be freed, and continued to drive south to link up with other U.S. units pushing north from Frankfurt. Then moving back to Limburg, it attacked east and north to help encircle the Ruhr Valley, after which it veered to the right and raced eastward with three combat commands abreast to encircle Leipzig and reach the Mulde River on 15 April. By dawn on the next day, it had crossed the river, seized Colditz, and liberated another POW camp before being ordered to hold in place. Four days later, it turned its positions over to the 2nd and 69th Infantry Divisions and shifted south to Czechoslovakia . At the war's end, CCA had advanced to Karlsbad while the remainder of the division was poised further south for an attack through Pilsen. Shortly after VE Day, the Division moved back to Germany where it performed occupation duty north of Nurmberg in the vicinity of Bayreuth until its return to the United States.

A howitzer of the 73rd AFA Battalion carefully maneuvers a street in Limburg, March 27, 1945.

Task Force Schantz of the 9th Armored Division crosses the Naumburg Bridge.

One of the most dramatic and retold stories of World War II: the 9th Armored's taking of the Ludendorff Bridge at Remagen.

New Pershing tanks for the 9th Armored, 1945.

10th Armored Division

BATTLE CREDITS

Ardennes   Rhineland   Central Europe

COMMANDERS
(World War II era)

July 1942 to July 1944	MG Paul W. Newgarden
August 1944 to May 1945	MG William H.H. Morris, Jr.
June 1945 to October 1945	MG Fay B. Prickett

COMPONENT UNITS

As of September, 1944: 3rd, 11th and 21st Tank Battalions; 20th, 54th and 61st Armored Infantry Battalions; 419th, 420th and 423d Armored Field Artillery Battalions. *High Commands*: First Army and Seventh Army.

The "Tiger" Division was activated at Fort Benning, Georgia, on 15 July, 1942 and departed in June of the following year to participate in Tennessee maneuvers. Upon termination of the maneuvers in early September, 1943, it transferred to Camp Gordon, Georgia, where on 14 July, 1944, the eve of its second anniversary, it was plunged into sudden mourning at the untimely death in an airplane crash near Chattanooga, Tennessee, of its popular commander, Major General Paul W. Newgarden, together with Colonel Renn Lawrence, the Commander of Combat Command "B". Several weeks later, it departed for Camp Shanks, New York, and embarked for France on 13 September, being the first Armored Division to sail from the United States directly to the European mainland.

10th Armored Division World War II Combat History

The 10th Armored Division entered combat near Mars La Tour, France, on 2 November, 1944 and on the 15th of the same month, joined in the fight to reduce the fortress city of Metz. Crossing the Moselle to the north in a wide encircling sweep, it attacked northeast and southeast in a two-pronged drive, reached the Saar River, and on 19 November, crossed into Germany at Eft. When the Ardennes offensive was launched, it rushed north to help with the German tide and, while CCB blocked the northern and eastern approaches to Bastogne by organizing defenses at Nomile, Longville and Bres and joined the 101st Airborne Division later in holding Bastogne, the remainder of the 10th Armored "Tigers" rammed into the enemy along the southern hinge of the Bulge in the vicinity of Berdorf and Echlarmach. Following a rest after the Bulge, the Division returned to the front on 22 February and helped to clear the Saar-Moselle Triangle. It then swung north and captured the historic city of Trier on 2 March after which, driving southeast through the Palatinam, it captured St. Westful on the 19th, raced through Kaiserslautern on the 20th, took Landau on the 22nd, and reached the Rhine that same day. It crossed the river at Worms on the 28th, passed through the 44th Infantry Division at Mannheim on the 30th and, on the 31st, drove into Heidelberg, which had been declared an open city. Racing east and bypassing Heilbronn enroute, it veered south and seized Crailsheim on 7 April. Isolated at this location deep in the enemy's rear and faced with daily increasing pressure and mounting casualties, it withdrew a short distance to the north on the 11th, then attacked back to the west, seizing Chringon on 13 April. Launching a new drive to the south from this point, in rapid order it captured Schwaebisch Hall on the 18th, Gaildorf on the 19th, Kerchheim on the 20th, and reached the Danube on the 22nd. It then swung east toward Ulm, taking the cathedral city on the 25th. At Ulm it turned south once more and, attacking into the rugged Alps on two parallel routes, it reached the Mitsenwald area when the war ended. Following VE Day, the Division performed occupation duty in the Garmisch-Partenkirchen area until it departed, on 12 September, for Marseilles, France, from which it sailed for home. Upon debarkation in the United States, it was inactivated at Camp Patrick Henry, Virginia, on 15 October, 1945.

In the spring of 1945 the 10th Armored rolled across Germany. Here a tank blasts snipers along the line of advance.

A tank of CCB of the 10th Armored, with infantry support, moves cautiously through a town, March, 1945.

November 24, 1944. Tanks of the 609th Tank Destroyer Battalion in Perl, Germany await orders to move up to the front.

April 7, 1945. Action in the "Bowling Alley" between Assamstadt and Crailsheim. A Tiger reconnaissance team in an M8 Armored Car fires on the enemy.

Infantry advances with 10th Armored tank support in the Meuberg area, April 17, 1945.

11th Armored Division

BATTLE CREDITS
Ardennes   Rhineland   Central Europe

COMMANDERS
(World War II era)

August 1942 to March 1944	MG Edward H. Brooks
March 1944 to March 1945	BG Charles S. Kilburn
March 1945 to September 1945	MG Holmes E. Dager

COMPONENT UNITS

As of September, 1944: 22nd, 41st and 42nd Tank Battalions; 21st, 55th and 63rd Armored Infantry Battalions; 490th, 491st and 492d Armored Field Artillery Battalions. *Higher Command*: Third Army.

The "Thunderbolt" Division was activated at Camp Polk, Louisiana, on 15 August, 1942, and, after completing required training and unit tests, participated in Louisiana maneuvers from June to September, 1943. It then transferred to Camp Barkeley, Texas, but was on the move again the following month. It took part in desert training and maneuvers in the Mojave from October, 1943 to February, 1944, after which it entrained for its new station — Camp Cooke, California. Several more months of combat preparations followed before the Division left for Camp Kilmer, New Jersey, on 10 September, 1944, and sailed on the 29th of that month for England.

11th Armored Division World War II Combat History

Arriving in England on 11 October, 1944, the Division trained on the Salisbury Plains for two months, then landed in France as the German Ardennes offensive was being launched. It headed east in a forced march on 20 December and, on Christmas, took over the rear area defenses along the Meuse River from Givet to Sedan. It was relieved the very next day and rushed to the vicinity of Bastogne where it entered combat near Remagne, Belgium, on 30 December, in an attack aimed at clearing the area west of Bastogne. Pushing north, it linked up with other US units along the Ourthe River near Houffalize on 16 January, pinching off a large number of the enemy. On 16 February, it launched a new attack eastward, penetrating the Siegfried Line at Peterskirche and taking Lutzkampen on the 17th. By the 22nd, it had cleared the enemy west of the Prum River and had reduced 30 square kilometers of the Siegfried defenses. Resuming its drive on 3 March, it captured Fleringen, Waller-sheim, and Budesheim in a matter of hours and, by mid-afternoon of the next day, had reached the Kyll River. It forced a crossing on 6 March, took the road center of Kilberg that night, and pushed on to link up with the 9th Armored Division along the Rhine on 9 March, then drove southeast toward Worms. It took Monsheim on the 20th and, on the 21st, overran the airfield south of Worms. It halted briefly, then crossed the Rhine at Oppenheim on 28 March, passed through the Main River bridgehead at Gross-Auheim on the 29th and attacked northeast, capturing Budin-gen on the 30th and reaching Fulda on the 31st. It bypassed Fulda, veered southeast through the Thuringean Forest, and crossed the Werra River at Wasungen on 2 April. Continuing the attack, it captured Steinbach-Hallenberg and Oberhof on the 3rd and, on the 4th, overran Suhl and seized Zella-Mehlis, the center of a large munitions complex which included the famous Walther Munitions Works. It raced on to take Meiningen on 5 April, halted to resupply, then resumed the attack on 10 April, capturing Coburg and Neustadt on the 11th, Kronach on the 12th, Kulmbach on the 13th, and the historic Wagnerian center of Bayreuth on the 14th. Continuing its push southeast, the Division crossed the Austrian border at Schwarzenburg on 26 April and by 6 May, had reached Klam when halted on orders. Two days later patrols made contact with the Russians at Amstetten just a few hours before official cessation of hostilities. A period of occupation duty in Austria followed VE Day until the Division was inactivated in September.

A column of 11th Armored Division tanks speeds through Mackazeuln on April 12, 1945.

11th Armored Division tanks advance; captured prisoners head
to the rear at Gallneukichen, May 4, 1945.

11th Armored tanks have a cold wait for orders to seize the town of Compogne, Belgium, January 2, 1945.

42nd Tank Battalion, CCA of the 11th, near Longchamps, Belgium.

Late December, 1944. The 11th Armored advances on Bastogne over the plains of Longchamps.

12th Armored Division

BATTLE CREDITS

Ardennes   Rhineland Central Europe

COMMANDERS

(World War II era)

September 1942 to August 1944	MG Carlos Brewer
August 1944 to September 1944	MG Douglass T. Greene
September 1944 to July 1945	MG Roderick R. Allen
July 1945 to August 1945	BG Riley F. Ennis
August 1945 to November 1945	BG Willard A. Holbrook

COMPONENT UNITS

As of September, 1944: 23rd, 43rd and 714th Tank Battalions; 17th, 56th and 66th Armored Infantry Battalions; 493rd, 494th and 495th Armored Field Artillery Battalions. *Higher Commands*: Third and Seventh Armies.

The "Hellcat" Division was activated at Camp Campbell, Kentucky, 15 September, 1942, and participated in Louisiana maneuvers from September to November of the following year. It then moved to Camp Barkeley, Texas and, while there, spent practically the entire month of June, 1944, away from station undergoing Division tests at Camp Bowier, Texas. It left Texas for Camp Shanks, New York, on 5 September, 1944 and sailed for Europe on the 20th of that month.

12th Armored Division World War II Combat History

The Division landed at Le Havre, France, on 11 November, 1944 and, following a bivouac of approximately two weeks in the vicinity of Auffay, moved east to Luneville on 29 November, closing in that area on 2 December. Initial commitment of division elements occurred on 5 December when the 493rd Armored Field Artillery Battalion, in support of the 44th Infantry Division, fired a mission from positions near Weislingen, France. Two days later the remainder of the Division, in relief of the 4th Armored Division, entered the line in the vicinity of Singling. In some of the bloodiest fighting of the war, it launched an attack against the German Rhine River bridgehead at Herrlisheim during the period 8-10 January and again 16-18 January. In each instance, after suffering severe casualties, it withdrew and successfully repulsed a strong follow-up counterattack. A brief rest toward the end of January followed, after which it resumed the offensive. Attacking south from Colmar on 3 February, it took Rouffach on 5 February and made contact with French units at that point to seal the Colmar Pocket and end German resistance in the Vosges Mountains. Then moving back to the 3rd Army sector, it joined in the drive east of the Moselle. It attacked southeast from Trier on 18 March, reached the Rhine near Grunstadt on the 21st, captured Ludwigshaven on the 22nd, seized Speyer on the 24th and made contact with the 14th Armored Division at Germersheim the same day. Crossing the Rhine at Worms on 28 March, it passed through the 3rd Infantry Division and pushed east to take Wurzburg on 3 April and Kitzigen on 5 April. After a brief halt, it turned south and in rapid order captured Neustadt on 16 April, Ansbach and Schwabach on 19 April, Dinkelsbuhl on 20 April and, on 22 April, seized a bridge across the Danube at Dillingen. Maintaining its rapid drive south, it took Landsberg (the site of Hitler's incarceration where he wrote *Mein Kampf*) on 27 April and, by 30 April, cleared the area between the Ammer and Wurm Seas. It continued the push into the "National Redoubt," crossed the Inn River and the Austrian border on 3 May, and took Kufstein the following day. It was relieved at this point and withdrew to the area of Heidenheim where it remained after VE Day and performed occupation duties until departure in November for the United States.

The 12th Armored Division at Camp Campbell, Kentucky, 1942.

Tanks of the 3rd Platoon, Company A, 23rd Tank Battalion, 12th
Armored in action near Strasbourg, France, January 17, 1945.

M3 tanks of the 12th Armored in training at Camp Campbell, 1942.

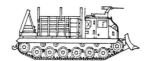

13th Armored Division

BATTLE CREDITS

Rhineland   Central Europe

COMMANDERS
(World War II era)

October 1942 to April 1945	MG John B. Wogan
April 1945 to November 1945	MG John Millikin

COMPONENT UNITS

As of January, 1944: 496th, 497th and 498th Armored Field Artillery Battalions; 24th, 45th and 46th Tank Battalions; and 16th, 59th and 67th Armored Infantry Battalions. *Higher Command*: Third Army.

The "Black Cat" Division was activated at Camp Beale, California, 15 October, 1942. It participated in the IV Corps Oregon maneuvers from September 15 to 8 November, 1943. Early in December of the following year, when orders for participation in the Oregon maneuvers had been cancelled, it transferred to Camp Bowie, Texas. The Division participated in a four-week field exercise, then was staged at Camp Kilmer, New Jersey from 14 January, 1945, until departure for Europe from New York. It arrived in France 30 January, 1945.

13th Armored Division World War II Combat History

After landing in France at Le Havre on 28 January, 1945, the Division spent approximately six weeks in the vicinity of Tates before moving east to forward assembly cities. While most of the Division stopped near Avricourt, the 7th Army Reserve Division Artillery continued toward the front to positions opposite Saarbrucken. There, on 18 March, having been given the mission of providing reinforcing fire for the 7th Army's attack on the Siegfried Line, its elements became the first units of the Division to enter combat, with "A" Battery of the 497th Armored Field Artillery Battalion dropping the first round on the enemy from positions near Spicheren, France. On 23 March, the artillery reverted to reserve and rejoined the Division which then moved, on 5 April, to Homberg near Canal and, as part of 3rd Army, prepared for relief of the 4th Armored Division. The relief was never affected, however, due to orders sending the Division north to 1st Army area where it was committed, on 10 April, in mop-up operations against enemy troops trapped in the Ruhr Valley. It crossed the Sieg River, pushed into Seigburg, and continued the drive to assist in wiping out the remainder of the Ruhr Pocket. It was in this encounter that the Division Commander, General Wogan, was seriously wounded on 14 April and replaced two days later by General Millikin. By 18 April, all enemy resistance in the Ruhr had ceased and the 13th Armored Division returned to 3rd Army control. Assembling in the vicinity of Parsburg, it moved out on 26 April, passed through the Danube River bridgehead at Ragensburg and fanned out toward the Isar River. Forcing a crossing at Platting on the 28th, it drove south with three combat commands abreast to smash across the Inn River on 2 May and into Braunau, Austria, the birthplace of Adolph Hitler. Relieved at this point, it withdrew into Germany where it performed occupation duty until it departed on 14 June to return to the United States for redeployment to the Pacific.

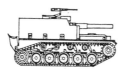

Adolf Hitler's Birthplace Captured By Division

THE BLACK CAT

VOL. 2 No. 2   13TH ARMORED DIVISION   GERMANY, MAY 15, 1945

13th's Final ETO Drive:

Victory In Bavaria

BATTLE Extra

Armoraiders Advance Into Austria To Wind Up Campaign In Redoubt; Danube, Isar And Inn Rivers Bridged

Braunau Obeys Surrender Edict At Last Moment

Braunau, Hitler's Austrian birthplace, was "captured" by a SHAIF broadcast on the morning of May 1 but was not actually taken by CC 'A' until several hours later.

The city, on the east bank of the Inn was taken without a fight but Gen. Augur's ultimatum to the garrison commander to "surrender or have the city destroyed" was not met until three minutes before the shell fired.

The Mayor of the Major W. A. Gray to given instructions to Braunau and deliver with the garrison. He came back with a note from the garrison commander which said: "I ask for mercy for the city of Braunau for its women and children. Our fight is against the Bolsheviks only, not against the Americans."

This reply was taken as a negative answer and Colonel Alfred E. Kastner's Division Artillery was ordered to start a bombardment of the city at 12 o'clock. At three minutes to 12, however, a delegation from Braunau, led by the Chief of Police, rowed rapidly across the river.

The delegation told Pfc. Harry Parker, Black Cat interpreter, that the civilians in Hitler's birthplace had convinced the army commander that last-ditch resistance in the face of overwhelming Yank power was hopeless, and that the city was now ready to surrender.

124th Armored Engineers then threw up a foot bridge over the debris of the regular bridge which the Germans had blown, and the 67th AIB's Baker Company, followed by Able and Charlie, crossed over and occupied the town.

Maybe These Krauts Thought M-C Needed More Personnel

An inkling that the end of the war was near came to one of the Message center teams of the 153rd Armored Signal Company a full five days before SHAEF announced it.

The men were busy as the proverbial one-armed paperhanger other when a German came into their building, queried "is this the Message Center?" and surrendered.

Nope, No Mayor; Only SS Officers

Two SS officers, who didn't know the law of falling bodies or just didn't give a damn, put on a brief, but spectacular show for men of the 24th Tank Battalion at Neu-Oetting shortly after the Combat Command "B" unit had forced the town's surrender.

The battalion pulled up at the banks of the Inn River just opposite Neu-Oetting on the night of May 1, and began negotiations for the surrender of the town. City officials were soon convinced of the futility of further resistance and turned the town over to CC "B" men.

All bridges across the river had been blown shortly before the 24th Tankers arrived and the only means of transportation was by boat.

(Continued on Page 5)

Racing through the valley of the historic Danube into the redoubt area which the Nazi armies had selected as their last-ditch stronghold, Black Cat Division armor stabbed across the Bavarian-Austrian border and wiped out enemy resistance in their zone of action shortly before the German Reich surrendered unconditionally and ended the European war.

Operating as part of the XX Corps of General George S. Patton's Third U. S. Army, 13th tankers, armored doughboys and armored artillerymen rolled 150 miles in a campaign that carried them across the Isar and Inn Rivers. Organized resistance in the Inn prisoners continued to pour in to 13th PWE's for several days, however.

More than 17,000 German prisoners were taken by the Division in the Bavarian campaign. Added to the estimated 20,000 PW's seized during the course of their Ruhr Pocket victory, Black Cat armoraiders wound up their ETO operations with a collection of some 37,000 Nazis in the prisoner bag.

More than 50,000 soldiers of the Hungarian Army also surrendered to the 13th Armored Division. These included the Hungarian vice-premier and the commander in chief of their army.

ACROSS THE DANUBE

On April 27, after the various units of the 13th had completed their long trek from the Ruhr Pocket area, Colonel Harold G. Holt's Combat Command "B" crossed the Danube River in the vicinity of Regensburg and pushed ahead to overrun Straubling. Task Forces McRae (for Maj. Robert McRae of the 24th) and Malone (for the 50th's Lt. Col. William F. Malone) made up the CC "B" lineup.

Because of driving rains and heavy mud, the roads leading up to the Danube bridges scheduled for use by CC "A" were almost impassable. After some delay however, Task

(Continued on Page 6)

The Bavarian-Austrian border region, shown in this German Chamber of Commerce photo...

German soldiers blew this bridge over the Inn before Black Cat soldiers could seize it intact, so 124th Engineers had to sweat out a foot-bridge to get 67th doughboys...

Page one of the May 15, 1945 *Black Cat*: "Racing through the valley of the historic Danube into the redoubt area which the Nazi armies had selected as their last-ditch stronghold, Black Cat Division armor stabbed across the Bavarian-Austrian border and wiped out enemy resistance in their zone of action shortly before the German Reich surrendered..."

THE BLACK CAT

VOLUME 2   13TH ARMORED DIVISION, AUSTRIA-GERMANY, TUESDAY, JUNE 5, 1945   NUMBER 4

Tank-Mounted Rocket Guns Work Out

ROCKET-FIRING TANKS were one of the ingenious devices in America's war arsenal that aided in the final rout of the German Wehrmacht. They're included in the Black Cat Division's stock of ordnance equipment. This picture was taken during a recent practice-firing session.

Memorial Rites Honor War Dead

Division Units Stage Colorful Parade in Eisenfelden

On the now peaceful ground where they had wrested less than a month before from the German Wehrmacht, members of the Division Wednesday morning bowed their heads in a Memorial Day tribute to their fallen comrades, and pledged themselves in their names to wage war unremittingly until for all time peace can be preserved.

The ceremony, held at Eisenfelden, Germany, began when General Wayland B. Augur mounted the dias, before which the colors and standards of the the Division's Battalions, and the battle-jacketed doughs of the 56th Armored Infantry Battalion were massed in impressive array.

As the last strains of the Ruffles and Flourishes sounded, all stood and joined Chaplain John T. Carey as he solemnly pronounced the Prayer for the Dead.

"Almighty and Merciful God, we of the 13th Armored Division, unite our hearts in humble prayer this Memorial Day. Enlightened by a holy faith and prompted by the rich traditions of our great land, we ask Thy boundless clemency upon the souls of our fallen comrades. In Days of world peril they advanced courageously against the foe. True to the spirit of high patriotism, they poured out their blood upon the altar of sacrifice. Dying, they live forever in the annals of the greatest nation in the world.

Eternal rest grant unto them, oh Heavenly Father, and let perpetual light shine resplendently upon their great souls. Through Christ Our Lord. Amen."

Then the assemblage was silent as the Strains of Taps resounded through the area, to be relayed by the hearts of those present over the graves of those who had died in the Ruhr Valley and in the final Bavarian Battles.

Throughout the Division, at the same moment, Memorial Day formations were being held, and a little of time was being silenced by the living in remembrance of the honoured dead.

The white-helmeted Division Band played the "Ave Maria," and Chaplain Sidney R. Crumpton rose to lead the assembled troops in a public plea for the return of world peace.

At the conclusion of Chaplain Crumpton's prayer, Sgt. Walter Avery sang the "Our Father."

The official tribute was ended with the playing of the National Anthem, but in the hearts of the men marching silently back to their billets was an eternal tribute.

Artillery Talent Scout Spots Two 13th 'Finds'

A former stage director and Hollywood talent promoter, now a Pfc. in the 497th Armored Field Artillery, has discovered two "finds" in the Black Cat Division and has already arranged a post-war contract for one of them.

The talent scout, Pfc. George West, contacted Hollywood last week and promoted a long-term film contract for Pfc. Francis La Cholla, a 19 year old Cat from Chester, Pa. According to West, La Cholla is a combination Mickey Rooney-Donald O' Connor prospect who is headed for big Hollywood stakes.

Negotiations are also under way between the Movie City and Bavaria to arrange a contract for Pfc. Elm Gibson, 19 year-old armored dough from Kansas City. Gibson used to be a drummer in Les Brown's Hollywood band.

(Continued on Page 2)

The CAT'S MEOW

TYPICAL GERMAN: When personnel men from the 497th AFA took over a house in Pfarrkirchen for billeting purposes, the family proclaimed with gusto their long-lived hatred for the Nazis and their time-honored allegiance to the Social-Democrat party. A few days later, some of the men decided to go fishing and started to dig for worms in the back yard. They came across a little bundle, which when opened, turned out to be a roll of Nazi swastikas and flags. They had been carefully covered to protect them from the elements.

PREMATURE BIRTH: A pregnant Austrian girl (about eight months gone, our reporters estimated) edged her way into the MG office at Braunau where Company B of the 67th holds forth. She reached her interpreter, Pfc. Harry Wagner and demanded to see the Military Governor. "One of your American soldiers is the father of my child," she dramatically announced. (Black Cat soldiers first arrived in Braunau on May 1).

THE LIARS CLUB: "We were talking about Hitler's death," wrote Mrs. C. Jones, Omaha, Neb, to Cpl. Charlie Jones of the 60th, one of the most famous fibbers in a GI uniform, "and one of the girls pointed out that Germany had lost its greatest liar. So I said that shouldn't worry Germany too much because they've got my husband over there now."

HEAVEN CAN WAIT: A Cat from the 153rd Signal Co. picked up this little item from a cousin of his who's sweating out the Philippines. When a supply column, following a mountain road that corkscrews to the top of a 2500-ft. peak on one of the islands, finally reached the pinnacle, the men noticed a huge sign: "If you want to go any higher than this, see the Chaplain!"

67th AIB Repatriates 5,000 Soviet PW's Liberated When 13th Drove Into Austria

More than 5,000 Red Army prisoners of war, who were liberated when CC 'A' units drove into Austria last month and who have since then, been transported to Russian-occupied Austria last week for further shipment home as part of the giant repatriation program now under way in the European theater.

The exchange was effected by a repatriation commission from Marshal Feodor Tolbukhin's 2nd Ukrainian Army. The commission arrived at the billeting point — an aluminum plant in Ransholen, Austria early last week and the repatriation was arranged after American and Russian medical officers had completed a joint examination of all the Red Army men.

Following the exchange of the Russian soldiers, arrangements were initiated to transport Russian civilian slave laborers under Division control in Austria into the Soviet occupied areas.

1st Lt. Joe B. Spaulding, 67th medical officer, and Capt. Stayton from the 83rd medical Battalion, worked with other American medical officers and with Russian medicos during the physical processing. The 1 Platoon of the 3rd Army's 55th Field hospital had set up a hospital in the plant so as to take care of some 400 of the ex-PW's suffering from malnutrition and disease. The Russians said that thousands from their prisoner group had died of starvation before the Division's units effected the rescue.

Out of 36 members of the Soviet commission, 17 were women. They included doctors, nurses and medical technicians. One of the women medical officers was a specialist in typhus and communicable diseases.

The able bodied Soviet soldiers were evacuated in 67th half-tracks to the vicinity of Furth, Austria, where the 80th Infantry Division is running a train to the Russian occupied area. Sick and wounded Red Army men were taken to a hospital train in 83rd Medical Battalion ambulances.

Capt. Nicolay Andreyevo, head of the Red Army repatriation commission, was enthusiastic in his praise for the 67th AIB personnel who took care of the Russian

(Continued on Page 2)

Gen. Wogan Salutes Black Cat 'Loyalty'

In a letter written on V-E Day to the personnel of the 13th A. D., Maj. Gen. John B. Wogan, former Division commander now being treated for battle wounds at Washington's Walter Reed Hospital, said that "although I am far removed from eighty-eights, screaming meenies and sniper bullets, my thoughts and spirit are with the officers and men of the splendid Black Cat Division on this day of glorious victory."

"It will always be a source of deep regret," the letter continued, "that I was deprived of the honor of leading the Division until the last shot was fired. I'd like to take advantage of this opportunity to express to all of you my sincere gratitude for the genuine loyalty and devotion shown me while I was your commander. From the bottom of my heart I send you my prayers and best wishes for your continued success and the efficient accomplishment of any and all tasks which may fall to your lot."

135th, 83rd Win Unit Plaques

The Meritorious Service Unit Plaque has been awarded to the 135th Ordnance Maintenance Battalion and the 83rd Medical Battalion Armored, for "superior performance of duty in the performance of exceptionally difficult tasks." The plaque, awarded under the provisions of WD Circular 345, gives the two battalions their authority to wear the award for its meritorious activities during the period from November 15, 1944 to May 15, 1945.

The Division departed the ETO for the U.S. nine days after this issue of *The Black Cat* was published.

14th Armored Division

BATTLE CREDITS

Rhineland   Ardennes   Central Europe

COMMANDERS
(World War II era)

November 1942 to July 1944	MG Vernon E. Prichard
July 1944 to September 1945	MG Albert C. Smith

COMPONENT UNITS

As Of October, 1944: 499th, 500th and 501st Armored Field Artillery Battalions; 25th, 47th and 48th Tank Battalions; 19th, 62nd and 68th Armored Infantry Battalions. *Higher Command*: Sixth Army Group and Seventh Army.

The "Liberator" Division was activated at Camp Chaffee, Arkansas, 15 November, 1942, and distinguished itself at that station, during the disastrous and record-breaking flood of May, 1943 by the assistance it rendered and the rescue operations it performed on behalf of the civilian population of Arkansas. It left Camp Chaffee in November, 1943 and participated in Tennessee maneuvers until January, 1944, after which it moved to Camp Campbell, Kentucky, where it remained until it moved overseas through Camp Shanks, New York, on 14 October, 1944.

14th Armored Division World War II Combat History

The 14th Armored Division landed at Marseilles on 29 October, 1944. Combat Command R, with little delay, moved east and went into the line in the Maritime Alps along the French-Italian border on 15 November. The remainder of the Division, meanwhile, marched north to Epinal, then assembled in the vicinity of Rambervillers on 21 November to launch an attack to the southeast. It took Shirmeck on 25 November, broke into the Alsatian plain on 27 November, then struck south in furious fighting to crack the German defenses at Gertwiller, Barr and Benfeld. A brief rest followed and, after regaining control of CCR which had moved up from the coastal Alps, the Division resumed the attack on 12 December, taking Hagenau, crossing the Moder River and, against increasing resistance, pushing through the Hagenau Woods to the Lauter River which separates France and Germany at that point. It bridged the river on 16 December and fought into Siegfried defenses but was forced to withdraw after suffering heavy losses. A few days later it was thrown into the Vosges Mountain defense line, taking over the sector from Bithe to Neunhoffen to help fill the gap created by units moving north to stem the German Ardennes offensive. It repelled a furious assault by six German divisions on 31 December and also stopped a similar attack the following month. The latter, launched on 9 January against the twin villages of Hatten and Rittershuffen, was later described by the Army Group Commander as one of the greatest defensive battles of the war. After a short rest in February, the Division jumped off again on 18 March, broke through the Siegfried Line on 23 March and, driving into the Rhine, took Gemerheim on the 24th. It crossed the river on 1 April, passed through the 3rd Infantry Division and, striking northeast, took Lohr on the 2nd and Gemunden on the 5th, liberated the POW camp near Hammelburg on the 6th, captured Neustadt on the 7th, and turned southeast to seize Lichtenfels and bridges over the Main River on 12 April. It then raced east to cut the Bayreuth-Nurnberg autobahn, swung south to take Creussen, then sped southeast again to reach Neumarkt by 19 April. Temporarily stopped by the enemy, it bypassed the city and drove on to cross the Altmuhl River on 24 April and reach the Danube on the 26th. It passed through the 86th Infantry Division bridgehead at Ingolstadt on the 27th, and fought south to the Isar River, over the Isar the following day, then continued its advance to reach the Inn River and establish bridgeheads at Jettenbach and Muhldorf on 2 May. It was relieved on 3 May and withdrawn north of the Inn River where it performed occupation duty until it departed for the United States.

14th Armored Division tank near Strasbourg, December, 1944.

Tanks of the 14th Armored Division liberate the POW camp at Hammelburg, April 6, 1945.

Infantry troops hop a ride on a 14th Armored Division tank.

Tanks of the 14th on the Bayreuth-Nurnberg autobahn, mid-April 1945.

Action outside Gambsheim.

16th Armored Division

BATTLE CREDITS
Central Europe

COMMANDERS
(World War II era)

July 1943 to August 1944	MG Douglass T. Greene
September 1944 to October 1945	BG John L. Pierce

COMPONENT UNITS
As of January, 1945: 395th, 396th and 397th Armored Field Artillery Battalions; 5th, 6th and 26th Tank Battalions; 18th, 64th and 69th Armored Infantry Battalions. *Higher Command*: Third Army.

The 16th Armored Division was activated at Camp Chaffee, Arkansas, 15 July, 1943, and remained there during the entire period of its training prior to overseas movement. Like the 20th Armored Division, it does not bear a nickname and was never allotted to the Regular Army subsequent to World War II. After undergoing the normal cycle of training and successfully completing all required unit and division tests and exercises at Camp Chaffee, it left for New York late in January, 1945, and sailed for Europe on 5 February.

16th Armored Division World War II Combat History

After arriving in Europe, the 16th Armored Division spent several weeks conducting additional training, first in France and then near Mainz, Germany. Finally, on 28 April, it began moving to Nurnberg where it assumed the security and patrol mission of the 80th Infantry Division in that city. On 29 April, the 23rd Cavalry Reconnaissance Squadron was detached and in turn attached to the 86th Infantry Division which, in conjunction with the 20th Armored Division, had launched an attack to the southeast to seize the city of Salzburg in Austria. Crossing the Isar River at Nieder-Neuching on 1 May, the 23rd cleared Aufhausen, Altewerding, Neuhausen, Papferding, Indorf, Pretzen, and Walpertshausen by evening. Then, having been reinforced by additional elements from the Division that night, it pushed out again to the south and east on 2 May, taking Haag and reaching the Inn River at Wasserburg. All units of the 16th Armored Division were relieved from attachment to the 86th Infantry Division at this point and rejoined their parent organizations on 4 May. The following day, the 16th Armored Division turned its security mission in Nurnberg over to the 4th Infantry Division and moved east to forward assembly areas in the vicinity of Waidhaus. From this location, it jumped off the next morning, passed through the 2nd and 97th Infantry Divisions at 0600 hours, and attacked down Highway 14 with Combat Commands B and R to seize the beer and munitions center of Pilsen. After overcoming scattered and sporadic resistance, it reached the center of Pilsen by 0800 hours and, by late afternoon, had cleared the city of all remaining significant resistance. The capture of Pilsen marked the deepest point of penetration into Czechoslovakia from the west. The 16th Armored Division remained in the vicinity of Pilsen following VE Day and performed occupation duty until it departed on 17 September for France, from which it sailed for the United States on 6 October, 1945.

May 6, 1945. The 16th Armored Division rolls into Pilsen, Czechoslovakia.

A 16th Armored Division soldier looks happy that the Division has seized one of the great beer capitals of the world. The 16th stayed in Pilsen after VE day on occupation duty.

Near Pilsen, with the war virtually over, the 16th Armored finally received new Pershing tanks with 90 mm guns.

20th Armored Division

BATTLE CREDITS
Central Europe

COMMANDERS
(World War II era)

March 1943 to October 1943	MG Stephen G. Henry
November 1943 to September 1944	MG Roderick R. Allen
September 1944 to October 1944	BG C. M. Daly
October 1944 to August 1945	MG Orlando Ward

COMPONENT UNITS
As of January, 1945: 412th, 413th and 414th Armored Field Artillery Battalions; 9th, 20th and 27th Tank Battalions; 8th, 65th and 70th Armored Infantry Battalions. *Higher Command*: Seventh Army.

The 20th Armored Division was activated at Camp Campbell, Kentucky, on 15 March, 1943 and, like the 16th Armored Division, bears no nickname and was not allotted to the Regular Army following World War II. Assigned an initial mission of conducting cadre and replacement training, it was directed, toward the end of the year, to attain combat-ready status. It immediately began a program of individual and unit training, followed in October, 1944, by a four-week maneuver conducted under its own direction. At the end of this phase of training, it began preparations for overseas movement, eventually leaving Camp Campbell on 18 January, 1945 and staging at Camp Miles Standish, Massachusetts. It sailed from Boston on 6 February, landing at Le Havre, France, on the 19th.

20th Armored Division World War II Combat History

The 20th Armored Division, after landing at Le Havre, France, on 19 February, 1945, assembled in the vicinity of Buchy, approximately 10 miles northeast of Rouen, where it processed equipment and underwent additional training. It then moved forward to assembly areas near Aachen, Germany, on 31 March and was assigned a reserve mission. On 3 April, the 33rd Cavalry Reconnaissance Squadron took over positions on the west bank of the Rhine near Horren from elements of the 97th Infantry Division but was relieved later that day and returned to the Division. The following morning, Division Artillery was ordered to the front to provide reinforcing fire for the 82nd and the 101st Airborne Divisions north of Cologne. Six days later, the 20th Armored Division moved south, then crossed the Rhine at Bad Godesburg and went into an assembly area in the vicinity of Lagenderback, north of Limburg, preliminary to joining in mop-up operations in the Ruhr Valley. This commitment failed to materialize, however, and it moved southeast of Wurzburg to the Ochsenfurt-Kitzingen area, then on 25 April jumped off in an attack toward Munich. The first direct encounter with the enemy occurred later that day when a group of German fanatics displayed a white flag of surrender at the town of Dorf in an effort to draw Task Force Campbell into a trap. Dorf was leveled and the advance continued. On 27 April, the Division reached the Danube, crossed it the following day, and by evening had seized Grasse-Nobach, north of Munich. It pushed into Munich on the 29th, after smashing the furious resistance of the largest SS Barracks in Germany and a Wehrmacht antitank school, then, on the next day, assisted the 3rd, 42nd and 45th Infantry Divisions in securing the city. Turning east from Munich it continued the attack, seized a dam over the Inn River at Wasserburg on 3 May, established a bridgehead at that point, then pushed on to cross the Salzach River on 4 May and enter Salzburg. It held there on orders and remained in this position until the end of the war, then performed occupation duty in the vicinity of Salzburg after VE Day until it left for France on 10 June to return to the United States for redeployment to the Pacific.

20th Armored Division M7 "Priest" patrols in a Bavarian town, clearing the last pockets of German resistance, late April, 1945.

20th Armored Division tanks seize Munich, where their reception was "more like a liberation than a conquest." German civilians, like these shown here, showered the tankers with flowers and wine.

A repair and maintenance stop for the 20th on the drive toward Munich.

Tank Destroyers

Allied armor engagements with German forces in 1940 and 1941 spurred the American command not only to upgrade the quality and quantity of U.S. tanks, but also to think in terms of antitank strategies and weapons. This concern led to the formation of a separate tank destroyer force. The Tank Destroyer Tactical and Firing Center was activated on December 1, 1941 at Fort Meade, and within three months was redesignated the Tank Destroyer Command and moved to Temple, Texas. In May of 1942, instruction began at the Tank Destroyer School; in October the School established an Officer Candidate School, which was later joined with the armor OCS at Fort Knox. By the summer of 1942, the Tank Destroyer Command was renamed theTank Destroyer Center and had relocated to Camp Hood, Texas. The Tank Destroyer Center was deactivated on November 10, 1945.

An M10 Tank Destroyer crew in the Rhineland begins repairs on the vehicle as the commander keeps a wary eye on the horizon.

An M36 Tank Destroyer keeps its gun barrel pointed down a Rhineland street.

An M10 Tank Destroyer fires its 76mm gun at German pill-boxes across the Sauer River from Echternach, Luxembourg, February 7, 1945.

An M10 Tank Destroyer with a hedgerow device in front.

An M18 Tank Destroyer patrols through Bavaria.

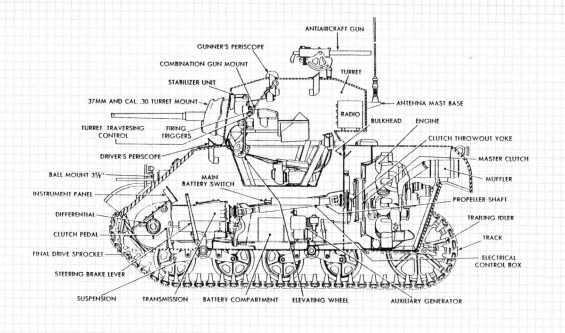

M3A1 LIGHT TANK

Crew	4
Length, Gun Fwd.	14' 10"
Width	7'4"
Height	7'6"
Combat weight	28,500 lbs
Engine	Continental W970-9A, 250 h
Speed	36 MPH
Range	70 miles
Armament	37mm M6 gun; 3 .30 cal. MGs

M4A2 MEDIUM TANK (SHERMAN)

Crew	5
Length, Gun Fwd.	19.41'
Width	8.58'
Height	9'
Combat weight	70,200 lbs.
Engine	GM 6046
Speed	25 MPH
Range	100 miles
Armament	75mm M3 gun; 1 .50 cal. MG; 2 .30 cal. MG

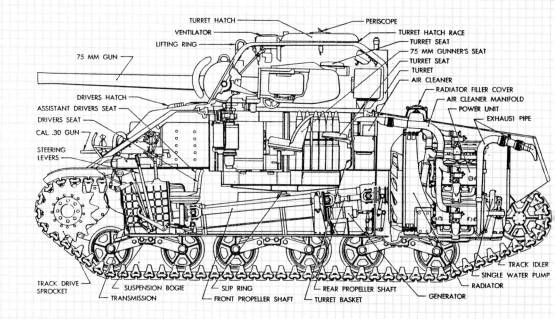

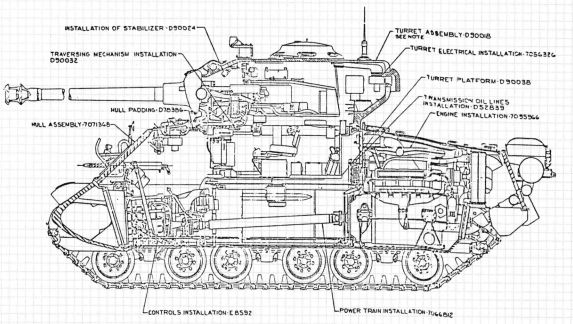

M4A3 MEDIUM TANK (SHERMAN)

Crew	5
Length, Gun Fwd.	24.75'
Width	9.83'
Height	9.75'
Combat weight	74,200 lbs
Engine	Ford GAA
Speed	26 MPH
Range	100 miles
Armament	76mm gun 1 .50 cal. MG; 2 .30 cal. MG

M24 (CHAFFEE)

Crew	5
Length, Gun Fwd.	18'
Width	9'8"
Height	8'2"
Combat weight	40,500 lbs.
Engine	2 Cadillac 44T24 V8s
Speed	34 MPH
Range	100 miles
Armament	75mm M6 gun; 1 .50 cal. MG; 2 .30 cal. MG

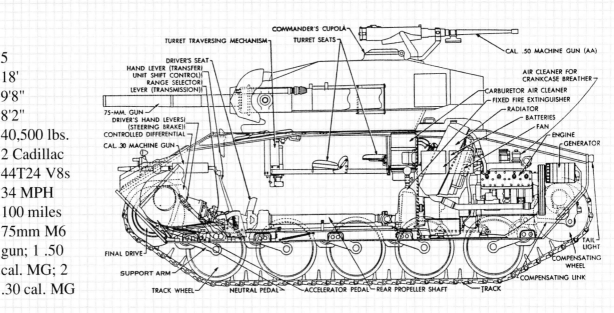

M26 (PERSHING)

Crew	5
Length, Gun Fwd.	27'11"
Width	11'6"
Height	9'1"
Combat weight	82,200 lbs.
Engine	Ford GAF
Speed	20 MPH
Range	92 miles
Armament	90 mm M3 gun; 1 .50 cal. MG; 2 .30 cal. MG

M46 (PATTON)

Crew	5
Length, Gun Fwd.	27.75'
Width	11.5'
Height	10.41'
Combat weight	97,000 lbs.
Engine	Continental AV-1790
Speed	30 MPH
Range	80 miles
Armament	90 mm M3 A1 gun; 1 .50 cal. MG; 1 .30 cal.

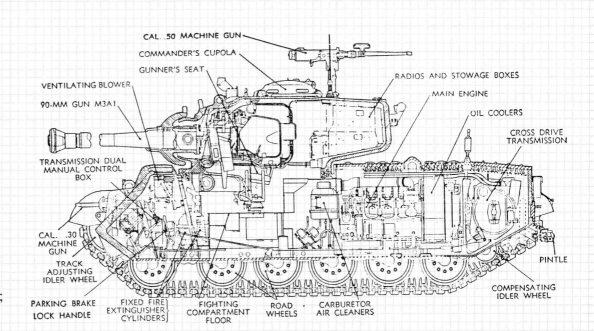

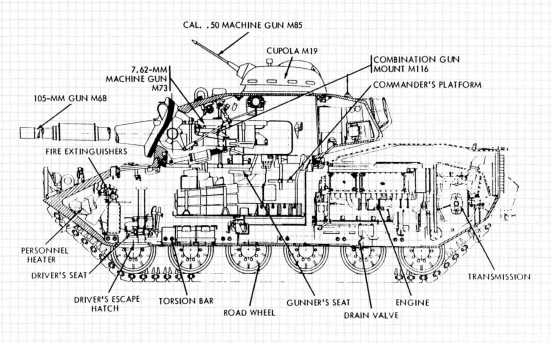

CAL. .50 MACHINE GUN M85

CUPOLA M19

7.62-MM MACHINE GUN M73

COMBINATION GUN MOUNT M116

COMMANDER'S PLATFORM

105-MM GUN M68

FIRE EXTINGUISHERS

PERSONNEL HEATER

DRIVER'S SEAT

DRIVER'S ESCAPE HATCH

TORSION BAR

ROAD WHEEL

GUNNER'S SEAT

DRAIN VALVE

ENGINE

TRANSMISSION

M60 MBT

Crew	4
Length, Gun Fwd.	30'6"
Width	11'11"
Height	10'7"
Combat weight	46,266 Kg
Engine	Continental
	AVDS 1790
Speed	30 MPH
Range	310 miles
Armament	105mm gun
	1 .50 cal MG
	1 .30 cal MG

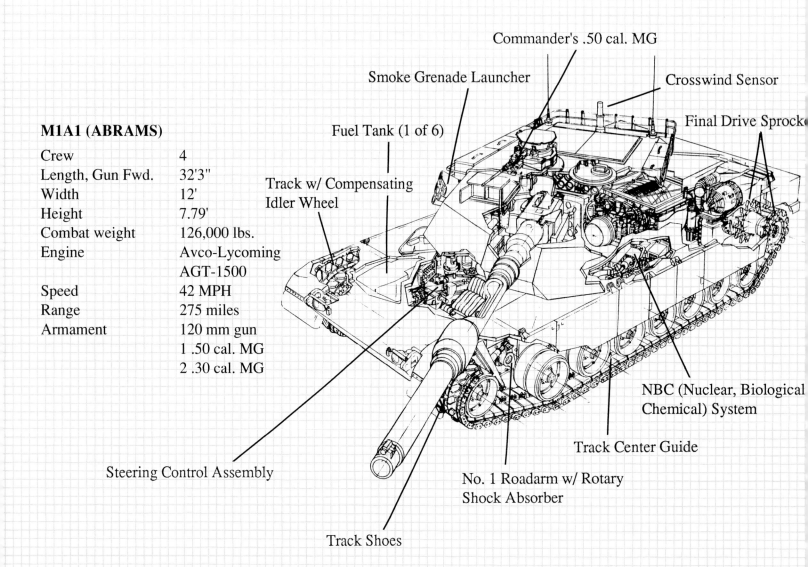

Commander's .50 cal. MG

Smoke Grenade Launcher

Crosswind Sensor

Final Drive Sprock

Fuel Tank (1 of 6)

Track w/ Compensating Idler Wheel

NBC (Nuclear, Biological Chemical) System

Track Center Guide

Steering Control Assembly

No. 1 Roadarm w/ Rotary Shock Absorber

Track Shoes

M1A1 (ABRAMS)

Crew	4
Length, Gun Fwd.	32'3"
Width	12'
Height	7.79'
Combat weight	126,000 lbs.
Engine	Avco-Lycoming
	AGT-1500
Speed	42 MPH
Range	275 miles
Armament	120 mm gun
	1 .50 cal. MG
	2 .30 cal. MG

AH1 COBRA

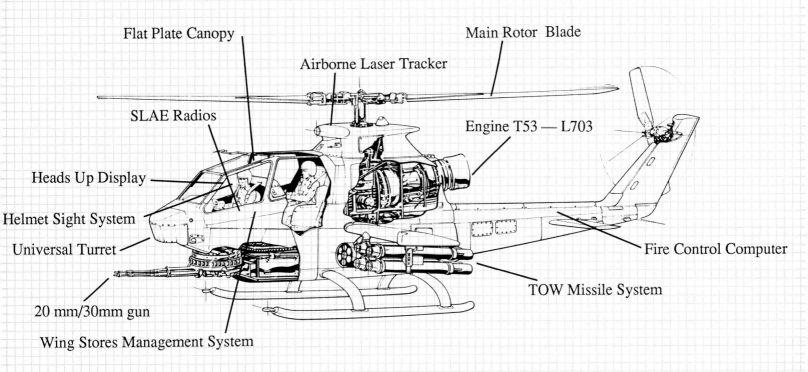

Flat Plate Canopy

Airborne Laser Tracker

Main Rotor Blade

SLAE Radios

Engine T53 — L703

Heads Up Display

Helmet Sight System

Universal Turret

Fire Control Computer

20 mm/30mm gun

TOW Missile System

Wing Stores Management System

AH-64 APACHE

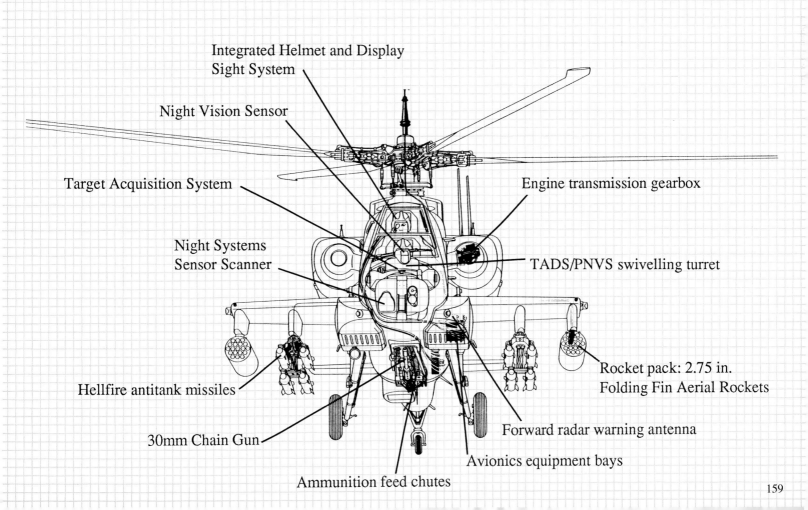

Integrated Helmet and Display Sight System

Night Vision Sensor

Target Acquisition System

Engine transmission gearbox

Night Systems Sensor Scanner

TADS/PNVS swivelling turret

Hellfire antitank missiles

Rocket pack: 2.75 in. Folding Fin Aerial Rockets

30mm Chain Gun

Forward radar warning antenna

Ammunition feed chutes

Avionics equipment bays

PHOTO CREDITS